SENS-PLASTIQUE

To Susan
with all good wishes
and the center of all things
Irving W.
04/06/02

OTHER BOOKS BY MALCOLM DE CHAZAL: A SELECTION

Pensées, seven volumes (Mauritius, 1940–45)
Sens-Plastique I and *II* (Mauritius, 1945 and 1947)
Sens-Plastique (Paris, 1948)
La Vie filtrée (Paris, 1949)
L'Ame de la musique (Mauritius, 1950)
La Pierre philosophale (Mauritius, 1950)
Petrusmok (Mauritius, 1951)
Le Livre de conscience (Mauritius, 1952)
La Bible du mal (Mauritius, 1952)
L'Evangile de l'eau (Mauritius, 1952)
Le Sens de l'absolu (Mauritius, 1956)
Sens Magique (Tananarive, 1957)
Apparadoxes (Mauritius, 1958)
Poèmes (Paris, 1968)
L'Ile Maurice: proto-historique, folklorique et légendaire (Mauritius, 1973)
L'Homme et la connaissance (Paris, 1974)

Sens-Plastique
by
Malcolm de Chazal

**Edited and translated from the French
with an Introduction by Irving Weiss**

NEW YORK 1979

ACKNOWLEDGEMENTS

Selections from this book have appeared in *Chicago Review, Contact*, and *SUN*.
An earlier edition of this volume, entitled *Plastic Sense*, was published in 1971 by Herder and Herder (New York).

Sens-Plastique copyright © 1948 by Editions Gallimard

English language translation and Introduction copyright © 1979 by Irving Weiss

Cover art copyright © 1979 by Malcolm de Chazal

Copyright © 1979 by SUN

All rights reserved. No part of this publication may be reproduced or transmitted in any form by any means, electronic or mechanical, including photocopy, recording, or any information storage and retrieval system without the written permission of the publisher, except in the case of brief quotations embodied in critical articles and reviews. For information address SUN, 456 Riverside Drive, New York, NY 10027.

Printed in the United States of America

Second revised and corrected edition

Library of Congress Cataloging in Publication Data

Chazal, Malcolm de, 1902-
    Sens-plastique

    First ed. (1971) published under title: Plastic sense.
    I. Weiss, Irving, 1921-   II. Title.
PQ3989.C42S413   1979   848'.9'1402   79-25078
ISBN 0-915342-29-4

The publication of this book is supported by grants from the National Endowment for the Arts in Washington, D.C., a Federal agency, and the New York State Council on the Arts.

Introduction

The French writer, painter, and mystic thinker Malcolm de Chazal is little known outside his native island of Mauritius except for echoes of the clamor in Paris that greeted the Gallimard edition of his *Sens-Plastique* in 1948. This volume, his literary masterpiece, containing about two thousand unnumbered aphorisms, pensées, and longer reflections, was introduced by Jean Paulhan as an original work of genius, a poetry of rude supernatural precision. It was enthusiastically praised by André Breton for its revolutionary oracular truthfulness of statement and as a type of writing without historical precedent. A controversy ensued in the pages of *Figaro*, *Combat*, and other journals about whether Chazal's aphorisms presented an occultist's view or constituted a new form of surrealism, whether Chazal was writing poems or prose, whether his meanings were to be taken figuratively or literally. After the Gallimard publication in 1949 of *La Vie Filtrée*, a collection of essays explaining the principal ideas of *Sens-Plastique* and elaborating on his methods of thinking and writing, Chazal continued to occupy the literary stage for a while. Since the 1950s, however, although several later books of his have been published in Paris, most of his writings were issued only under a Madagascan or Mauritian imprint, and Chazal has been largely forgotten abroad.

Malcolm de Chazal comes from a French family that established itself on the island of Mauritius in the 18th century. He was born in Vacoas, Mauritius, in 1902, and except for six years at Louisiana State University at Baton Rouge, where he received an engineering degree, he has remained most of the time in Mauritius. He worked as an engineer on sugar plantations and later for the Office of Telecommunications, retiring at the age of 55. By his own admission, an uneventful life, but teeming with ideas and images that began to take written form in 1940 with the publication in Mauritius of the first volume of his *Pensées*. In the next five years five more collections of *Pensées* appeared, consisting in all of almost 3000 numbered passages. In 1945 a seventh volume of *Pensées* appeared, bound with another collection of aphorisms entitled *Sens-Plastique;* and two years later a separate *Sens-*

Plastique, volume II, appeared. It was this latter volume on which the Gallimard edition was based and that brought Chazal into prominence in France.

The *Pensées* and the Mauritian editions of *Sens-Plastique* have long been out of print. According to the Mauritian writer Camille de Rauville, who quotes from the *Pensées* in his *Chazal des Antipodes*, the passages are written for the most part in the moralist tradition of La Rochefoucauld, and it was only in the last two volumes of the *Pensées* that Chazal's mind and style began to adopt the aphoristic mode of sensuous intuition that is fully distinctive of his greatest achievement, *Sens-Plastique*.*

What struck Jean Paulhan and André Breton, Denis Saurat, Leopold Sedar-Senghor, and W. H. Auden as astonishing and unclassifiable about *Sens-Plastique*—to name some well-known literary figures who have written about it—can perhaps be illustrated by a few excerpts.

Half-opened petals give the flower an adenoidal look.

We know the halls of the eye like welcome visitors but we live in our mouth.

Any man who acts singly in the press of a mob will get trampled. Shifting into reverse while making love can kill you.

Immediately before it falls, water turns into a living being as if a person's soul had just slipped into it: look at the way it bends and twists, writhing in desperation. (What if you threw a not quite cold corpse out of an airplane—would the dead awaken?...)

Our surprise in reading these observations carries with it a certain uneasiness, a quizzical amazement at their meanings. If the author's imagination and literary artistry are his prime movers

---

* Chazal des Antipodes: Approche et Anthologie (Les Nouvelles Editions Africaines, 1974), an interpretive anthology of Chazal's writings commemorating the author's 70th birthday, with a preface by the poet Léopold Sédar-Senghor, President of Senegal.

here, then these are probably "poems"—but there is an inscrutable self-assurance in them that at the same time leads us away from their inventiveness and towards the objective world they describe. And this is where Chazal's status as an illuminatus begins: he is telling us things that we can't completely follow unless we decide to trust his revelations, trust them even when we fail to understand him completely. In the examples given above, the comparison between flower and face can be recognized wryly and then dismissed as a fanciful truth, on the level of a conceit. The second comparison, however, merges analogy with identity, reminding us that we live "inside" our own bodies. In the third example, about crowds and sexual love, Chazal is making a more comprehensive statement about the self and otherness. In the last one we are on the verge of comparison as a metaphysical method, no longer figurative only, a method based on some secret sense of animistic correspondences. When we consider that *Sens-Plastique* is made up of thousands of such comparisons, it seems likely that for all his strange sense of humor, Chazal intends to be taken seriously and means likeness to be understood as a form of identity: the adenoidal look of the half-opened petal is just as real as it is apparent.

One can make something too much of Chazal's engineering training, but it should be kept in mind when we consider the kind of information *Sens-Plastique* contains. The uniqueness of its material and style seems more understandable if we consider the passages to be prose statements of fact, that is, "scientific" observations, rather than prose poems, as they are sometimes taken to be. They are also science fictions, extensions of present knowledge, visionary statements, verbal accounts of a sensory investigation of man and nature, mostly visual but frequently deriving from the other senses. Chazal thinks of his writing as a form of picturing in words that demonstrates what he perceives. He has remarked that after Georges Braque read *Sens-Plastique*, he wrote to say that the book was "beyond literature," essentially an *album d'images*, and that Chazal should take up painting. He did not follow Braque's suggestion until 1954. Since the 1960s he has had exhibitions in France and England. The afterword in Camille de Rauville's commemorative volume represents the opening address by Léopold Sédar-Senghor at an exhibition of Chazal's paintings,

November 22, 1973, at the Musée Dynamique de Dakar. They are vivid, simplified renditions of the Mauritian landscape, especially its flora and fauna, seen as glowing metamorphic emblems.

The mental and spiritual energy that filled the pages of *Sens-Plastique* led in one direction towards painting and in another towards a number of books which systematized Chazal's views as a mystical thinker.* A third direction led Chazal towards poetry proper, indicating that only as a colorful, sensuous, impassioned expression in words should *Sens-Plastique* be considered poetry. Chazal did not find inappropriate W. H. Auden's inclusion of excerpts from it in *The Viking Book of Aphorisms*. But the fact that he also wrote the gnomic verses of *Sens Magique* as a companion volume in title and subject matter showed his intention to distinguish the form of the aphorism from that of the poem.**

The passages in *Sens-Plastique* consist of assertions *about* the ways in which all the elements in nature relate to each other, and the language is intended to be simply declarative. Chazal is an empiricist reporting on events in nature, noting correspondences for their own sakes. He recreates their essential unity by looking at "term" one through the eyes of "term" two, that is, by intuitively becoming the second term himself. He is not working with figurative language, metaphors, or similes, but with the things themselves. The writing reads like poetry because it enlarges our sense of possibility, but Chazal here keeps crossing the border between literature and prophecy, language and the ineffable, for the whole enterprise of *Sens-Plastique* is dedicated to descrying in nature's oneness exactly how everything may be understood as everything else. Those of us who still find it literature—communicative as well as expressive and symbolic—can none the less think of it as factual writing because, often enough, its psychological truthful-

---

*Notably *Petrusmok* (1951), a spiritual history of Mauritius "written" in the rocks and mountains of the island, and *L'Homme et la Connaissance* (1974), in which he explains the harmony of the universe according to a magical physics based on movement, the living, human characteristics of all evidence as a form of experience.

**Later poems of the same kind appear in *Apparadoxes* (1958) and *Poèmes* (1968).

ness and accuracy of perception are so impressive. When we are not impressed there is often a doubt whether we haven't understood rather than that Chazal has got his psychic optics or his arcane physics wrong.

Chazal developed this personal mode of perception slowly, after years of observing physical materials, colors, light effects, time relations, and situations in space, as well as nature in all its forms, notebook in hand as he walked the beaches, fields, and woods of Mauritius. The minute precision of his perceptions of phenomena gives him a semi-professional voice when his subject lies in astronomy, physics, physiology, ethology, horticulture, fashion design, or other supposedly circumscribed fields, in each of which, however, he sometimes speaks with the accents of a Goethe or a Rudolph Steiner: he will not be stopped from unifying science even at the risk of hermeticism. The biographical information that Chazal has never been reluctant to divulge, that one uncle was a Swedenborgian and another a friend of Claude de Saint-Martin, satisfies some of our curiosity about inherited influences. And critics have of course long since noted that he has brought to some kind of fruition the speculative poetics of Baudelaire and Rimbaud, since Chazal has got closer than any other visionary man of letters to naming the connections between forces and forms, and in one example after another to defining the laws by which correspondences in nature are determined. He has, however, refused to be identified with any previous person or system. To the extent to which Chazal propounds his own system, which he has referred to as *Unisme*, in his writings of the past thirty years after the publication of *Sens-Plastique*, he claims to have received a unique revelation as the crowning result of the intuitive methods he pursued in the creation of his masterpiece.

The casual reader would refuse to give *Sens-Plastsique* a second glance if Chazal's distinctiveness were merely a matter of his coining a new system—there are too many already—except that so many of his minted pieces look solid and ring sound.

> *High heels elongate the movement of legs toward the torso, so that the lower part of women's bodies ends in a birdlike gait at the same time as the upper part of their bodies develops an elephantine waddle. It is impossible to improve any part of the human body arti-*

ficially without detracting from the natural grace of some other part.

The scurrying snake sculls with his whole body—which gives him wings. The fish flopping in the grass sculls while running—which gives him legs. Rippling and rolling water flies higher in space.

With branches, stems, petals, flowers, and fruit, it is never a question of right or left because the plant world offers us no cardinal point of view. The only apparent direction is that every branch stands out like a left arm when it looks at us. If it were otherwise we wouldn't see space head-on as we do but in all directions at once whenever we turned its way. If nature gave us an immediate sense of right and left whenever we looked at it, space would simply lie askew to our open eyes.

According to Chazal's scroll of pictures as it unrolls passage after passage in no predetermined order—observations of air, noses, sex, jewelry, insects, chronology, race, generations, flowers—the natural and the moral world are the same, one makes no sense without the other despite their conventions of distinctness. *Sens-Plastique* tells us that it is man's incapacity to encompass the perception of both worlds in one view that creates absurdity and not any gap between the worlds. *Sens-Plastique* provides us with microscopic and telescopic, infra-red and ultra-violet camera glimpses of this essential unity; and Chazal's genius lies in his choice of ambush for each view. Hence the form he chose for a collected display: a sequence of separate statements. Anyone can argue convincingly that reality lies behind appearance, but it is not our intellects that need convincing. Poetry, music, and painting argue even better by convincing our imaginations. But one still longs to perceive this reality and *Sens-Plastique* reports that it is indeed perceptible and flashes it before us.

The green of leaves at early dawn creates in us a sensation of mauve. The eye sees green but the soul sees mauve. The interior realities of colors are absolutely unrelated to their exterior realities. The spiritual body is color-blind to the physical body. If we actually saw *blue in our soul at the same time as we saw blue in nature, the fusion would be so complete between mind and body that we would suffocate like the strangling man who must live on the pocket of air in his lungs.*

We never feel that nature is excessive in anything because color and form are so completely connected: button and buttonhole adjusted by divine fingers. Only manufactured objects strike us as excessive in one way or another, and this arises from the fact that either the buttonhole is too tight or the button "swims" in its moorings.

Chazal is at the opposite extreme of certain dehumanizing and anti-humanist tendencies in modern thought. Instead of disinfecting the natural world to keep it free from human influence and pathetic fallacies, he endows it with the features of that most enigmatic evidence of total symbolism—the human face and form: and at the same time enlarges the human face and form to universal proportions.

A mountain is a mountain, an automobile is an automobile, space is space—we are usually content to regard them as irreducible data, though in dreams and poems they may take on eyes and noses. But to the same degree an eye or a nose is never other than itself either, and although we may sometimes liken eyes to lakes and noses to peaks or bridges, we feel we have failed to grasp their spiritual quality. We suspect that eyes and noses may really be creatures with their limbs tucked under. There is something discrete and discontinuous about them. We should like to give them proper names. We don't really know the faces of people we know well, although from the gestures of their features we can begin to predict what they are likely to do. Everyone is also a poor amateur of the human face in general: the eyes express the soul, the nose expresses intelligence, the mouth, sensibility, and we leave it at that. The biographer analyzing the pictured representation of his subject in the frontispiece wastes his time; any reader can do as well after he finishes the book.

Chazal is the first of physiognomists because he has been able to trace the profile of each trait or feature by according it the dignity of a self, through a system of physiognomy treated as symbolic of the system of a universe in which everything is expressive of everything else. Each feature of the face and form modifies every other one; the human body itself is seen as a distributive form of the face, and each of the five senses is a symbol of the other. Chazal is so sensitive to the multiple implications of facial traits that he can read the personalities even of eyelashes more fluently than other physiognomists have been able to read the eyes and lips of personalities.

> *The eyelashes are the last of the features to grow old in man. Completely white eyelashes would deactivate the glance, and the eye itself would seem buried in the face just as the landscape seems to go underground after a snowfall. Only the mountain range of the nose would emerge in the heights of the face, an Alp in the naked plains and the featureless skies of the forehead.*

Since the human face and form lie at the center of his thought, it is not surprising that *Sens-Plastique* emerges as the work of a Christian thinker. We are led by statements in passage after passage back to the Incarnation as God's reminder to man that the correspondence between nature and man is complete, that all of nature is in the human face and form, polarized according to another scheme, and Christ a fusion of all things in time and space whom God exploded on the Cross.

> *Clothed as they are in gestures, our fingers hide their feelings. Our palms are as naked as light itself, communicating with the core of the brain. Hence the remarkable truthfulness of the lines of the hand and the miraculous imposition of Christ's hands—the palms leading to God—by which the Man-God works all his miracles. Do we not assign extraordinary importance to the gesture of blessing, to the total contact of the handshake, to the simple avowal of the hand raised in oath, to the useless washing of Pilate's hands (the palm being incapable of lying), and to the exposure of the Divine Palm on the cross, a palm whose supreme death throes shine like a lighthouse in the night of God's agony? Denude your gestures, your voice, and your step and you will feel yourself dressed in light.*

Chazal wrote *Sens Magique* to put the reader into the experience of sensing and perceiving the world as if through the author's own faculties rather than demonstrating and explaining the reality of it as he does in *Sens-Plastique:* the pithy verses of *Sens Magique* represent an existential version rather than an expository one. In *Sens Magique* the incident itself is presented as the magical moment embodied in verse, the laws of its occurrence are not discussed as they are in *Sens-Plastique*. It is the difference between

> *The white*
> *crying*
> *of the lilies*
> *chilled space.*
> *A red bird*
> *flew nigh*
> *and white burst its*
> *vessels.*
> *Summer was snowing.*

and

> *Light-dazzle jacks up space, adding a second storey to our view of things. Indeed, space keeps piling up levels as the breadth of our look increases. Imagine what would happen otherwise: our eyes would tend to see any sudden brilliance of light from behind rather than in front, in a sort of fourth dimensional perspective that would turn us all into seers.*

The difference between an aphorism or pensée and a poem is the difference between static and dynamic, an appeal to the reason to recognize and discriminate and one to the imagination to participate. An aphorism brings the subject to you, a poem takes you to it. What is confusing about *Sens-Plastique* is that it would seem to do both. We smile with pleasure at how Chazal has managed to super-realize his experiences but we still don't believe that the features are really animals; that flowers have faces; that the senses constitute an interconnecting system; that color is a moral condition of the world; that the sameness of the sun's light in physics, God's grace in theology, and the human look in psychology is a fact; and so on. And that is why Chazal wrote *Sens Magique:* to demonstrate by simplification, having gone as far as he could in *Sens-Plastique.* By using the form of verse, albeit an open form, he will put you inside the rhetorical vehicle and transport you to his magic land of the Sixth Sense lyrically.

The present selective translation of *Sens-Plastique* is intended to represent Chazal's great work by characteristic examples. It consists of the complete corrected text of my previous translation, *Plastic Sense* (1971), with numerous additions translated from the first half of *Sens Plastique.* It is hoped that the present volume will constitute the first installment of a complete translation of the original work. No attempt has been made to translate the original title, which the previous publisher's rendering, *Plastic Sense,* misrepresented over my objections and to the author's dismay. As Chazal himself has noted, he wanted *sens* to refer to the alchemy of the senses and *plastique* to call art into mind.

Although the reader may dip into *Sens-Plastique* at any point without missing the author's purpose—for only rarely does a particular subject fill successive passages—it should be noted that the passages tend to become longer as the work progresses, and the translation follows the order of the original. I have tried my best to capture the imagistic exactness of each selection by searching for an idiomatic and structural equivalent in English without departing too far from Chazal's stylistic intentions, and I have been greatly helped by the author's encouragement. He has been kind enough to say that my English reads more forcefully than the French. I hope that any advantage I may give to the reader of this translation has not been gained at the expense of misconstruing the original.

I am indebted to the State University of New York Research Foundation for some of the financial support that enabled me to translate this work.

Irving Weiss
Pine Bush, New York
November, 1979

The cerebellum and the cerebrum are respectively our human Senate and House where the body is the People, the senses are the Cabinet, and the nerves are the Federal Administration. In the body's democracy the soul is appointed President for life but without authority to dissolve Congress. All social democracies originate in the body's democracy and model themselves on it, with one difference: in its social form the individual matters most; in its physical form the only thing that ever matters is the common interest.

Water meanders on a completely smooth surface and toboggans down the glossiness of leaves.

Nature is the most beautiful of all picture books but its covers are shut tight. There can be no leafing through its pages unless we learn how to peel the layers off every plant, flower, and fruit as if they were onions or until we can absorb nature as a whole like an orchestra whose separate parts can be enjoyed in detail without sacrificing the total effect. Really to appreciate the flower's loveliness we would have to savor every streak, stripe, and splash of color, the texture, the down, the elastic marblings, every bit of light, dark, and patterning; the flesh and the spirit; the symbols, container, and setting; the stage, ramp, and wings; the orchestration of colors and marriage of forms; the architecture and the scenic design. But to get to the point of being able to pare the flower down minutely wouldn't the human eye first have to develop *planar* vision?

The feel of the neck of branches, of the mouth of the flower, of the belly of water, of the haunches of fruit. O leaves, your wet tongues.

Our fingers see the night like cats, but we never know it. In order to learn visual information from our fingertips we would have to shut our physical eyes into a psychic gaze as the blind do.

We are much more conscious of our backs at night than in the daytime. In the dark our vision is more psychic than physical. It reaches out partially behind us, limiting what we can see straight ahead. In effect, total darkness and extreme fear make us recoil psychically even as we walk physically forward, creating a tension between our two modes of perception, like that in a tightly held elastic band. Anything we happen to collide against in the dark suddenly releases our extended double self so that it turns somersaults like an elastic band bounding up and over itself after the stretched ends have been simultaneously released.

Old men are no more capable of recruiting new gestures than new ideas. Age is through with innovation, every apparently new gesture in the aged being little more than a magnified tic.

The idealist walks on tiptoe, the materialist on his heels.

The rapid displacement of perfumes in space cannot be measured only according to the physical laws of weight, volume and atmospheric pressure. There are also the unknown laws of olfactory attraction, like the individual magnetism of the nose. A strong magnet pulls in iron fillings more swiftly than a weak one and the spaceships of our perfumes land more quickly on noses accustomed to air traffic than on provincial landing fields.

The plant uses the seed as a handbag.

Our organs nurse at our veins like infants at the breast. Blood is cellular milk. In fact, adult or aged man, whether we suck, chew, or gulp our mixture, our entire life on earth is a physiological activity at the sucking bottle of ourselves. Organically we are our own mother-and-child; and in the infinity of things, in Absolute Allness, we suck from God Himself.

Humored by the wind, the flower tosses its head, bowing on its stem like a woman who would give herself by refusing.

The eyes of flowers come in countless varieties of color, with the exception of green. If a plant had green eyes it would look insane, as if it had lost the wits of its way among the green leaves.

The act of love is a greyhound race of desire in which the pursuer collapses in front of the finish line, always short of his prey.

Light is a white flag on a yellow staff, ranging in whiteness from transparent to milky.

The arms of the tree are its shoulders, the shoulders of the quadruped are its legs, the torsos of birds are their hands, and the body of the insect is its fingers.

The ballerina dances in segments of movement, embodied arpeggios. Actually, even in nature, only flowing water makes every single movement with its whole body.

Tossed by the wind, flowers swivel their heads, fruits shake their hips, the creeper wriggles its whole frame. Seized from all sides by the hurricane, nature tries to uproot itself like a man struggling in a net.

Red is eternally pregnant with sunlight, miscarrying in pink, giving birth to yellow in orange, and to blue and mauve twins in garnet.

The eyes of blue flowers glance like featherweights and the eyes of red flowers like heavyweights. Imagine them boxing in the sunlight: obviously the reds will win. But let flowers fence with foils and yellow is international champion; or with sabers and white has no equal.

The miser pries out and picks at the pennies in his palm with clubfooted fingers on stilts.

Date palm. Corded rank of fruit: froggings on the sun's uniform. Palm frond fallen aslant over the trunk: shoulder sash. Ticks of glossy light on the leaf: "fruit salad." Knurl encircling the bark: waist sash. Treetop with its crown of leaves: plumed helmet. Exposed blade of heartwood: drawn sword. Trunk stiffly at attention. Planted soldier. Date palm.

Red is the universal hinge of color. If the sun were a rose-window, red would be at the hub.

A flower startled by the wind is like a woman whose lips are violated but melts a moment later into proffering them: bending forward with surprised and then pleased lips, the flower keeps turning its head, uncovering its mouth more and more to the tune of the wind's pressing demands.

The jerky and abrupt sound of the locomotive rises and falls according to pressure, followed by the level drone of the cars behind it. In the human voice, variation in pitch never affects timbre, which follows unchangingly behind.

A forced laugh makes the teeth look thin.

There is far north, *yonder*, far south, and *here* is the equator of words.

Flowers are both knowing and innocent, with experienced mouths but childlike eyes. They bend the two poles of life into a divinely closed circle.

The flower is a jumble of thighs, the sun's harem—the most Oriental thing imaginable.

Birds that wheel round and round and round in the blazing sun: their shadows on the ground box in the light.

The water that slides along oily surfaces of seaweed in full sunlight drags behind it the complementary pressure of light upon it, like horse and rider jerking together in full gallop.

The wind blows splayed out, legs and feet on water, arms outstretched everywhere else. Only a headwind blows like a chest in your face.

Every flower is a Mona Lisa following our glance whenever we look at it.

All flowers dress for the afternoon except the rose, whose shoulders overflow her haunches like a duchess trailing courtly robes.

We are more conscious of other people's noses than of any other part of the face. At the same time the nose is the feature in our own face we are least conscious of. Although we always sense the presence of our mouth, our nose seems a thing apart, so that we are much more aware of our neighbor's than of our own.

When the hurricane rips the air to shreds, the rain pastes the pieces together. When the fountain splinters water, the air glues it together.

Bearing children rounds out a woman's hips until she looks like one of those lovely old fruit trees back of the house.

A roomful of overexcited men or women: the men bray, the women cackle.

The mouth is the kind of fruit that must be eaten skin and all. Kisses you have to peel go down hard.

The flower is all woman: mouth, breasts and vagina—sex's three-in-one.

The bleat of an idiot's look.

The shimmer of noon above a liquid surface turns liquid itself and engulfs the water. The polished enamel of certain brilliant kinds of teeth inundates the lips until they overflow the face.

The thrilling softness of some voices seems to come from the nape of the neck like sweet notes that wind their way from the violin's drumbox.

Air is a ropeless swing as water is a seasaw with no fulcrum. But a look of the eye is a seesaw-swing without support or fixity. The eye's magnet moves it at a distance like the coachman sun driving his planetary cars in space.

Mounted in the elastic framework of space, the clouds are mobile canvases across which the sun lets his brush travel.

Animals exemplify whatever is natural, except when domesticated.

A man's heart lies in his genitality, a woman's genitality in her heart.

The toad suffused with fear swims as he runs, like a fish out of water that runs as it swims.

To hang on every word means to suck the eyes of the speaker.

Up to the point of disgust sweetness has no smell. Up to the point of bitterness salicity has no smell. At its own breaking point acidity turns tongue, nose, and stomach into a threefold sense of smell.

Grey puts the mind to sleep as brown the nerves. Whenever you feel indolent, give your mind a jolt of red and your nerves a dash of yellow.

Mauve flowers turn sunlight to twilight. Purple flowers fill the light with night.

Low clouds are the paperweights of the wind.

The blossoming flower, like a young girl whose pervading sexuality arches her loins, stands tall with upthrust bosom.

The mouth is the starting point of laughter, with the eye its destination. Long after the mouth is exhausted the eye continues to laugh.

Pride is enjoyed by the nape of the neck, vanity by the loins.

Light is never dirty except in the human glance.

No matter how plain or common her other features, a superb look in her eyes will turn any woman into a queen.

The emptied container of a sick man's voice.

The tempest in her haunches is a sign that a woman is beside herself with fury. An access of rage causes a hurricane in her breast.

The bosom is seated on the stool of the haunches with the lower limbs for legs. The first chair came into being as a symbol of the body.

The laughter of water at the springhead turns to sniggers as the river rolls on.

The beams of the eye can develop a kind of psychic force as circus trainers certainly know, who make use of it to overpower wild animals. Once we come to understand the inner mechanism of this force we will be able to use it on infinitely more sensitive forms of life, such as flowers. The flower held in our penetrating glance will then be set in motion by the transfusion of this invisible charge until it obeys us on its stem, dipping and bowing like a robot plane.

Hearing is a spectator who applauds with his eyes.

The plasticity of the mouth affects the plasticity of the face and even the most remote parts of the body: any stretched end of a rubber band reflects all the rest of it.

A white-throated flower looks larger than any other. Strikingly white teeth enlarge the mouth.

Sudden strong feeling thins the lips. Petals become tissue-fine blown by the wind.

The smoothest human skin roughens with age not unlike the gooseflesh of old natural leather.

Someday dresses will be woven of glass crystals, shaped into multicolored garments of an infinite variety of tones responding to every angle of light. And since color affects form, the hips and breasts of women will become elastic in the sun, making man throb with desire until he becomes passion's slave more than ever.

Pink is the plump color. Wear it to put on weight.

Red looks thin from top to toe but plump from side to side. Red tapers the bust and legs but widens the waist: hence its bracing effect on sexual desire.

Thick calves drag the hips downward into the legs. Slender legs elongate the waist upward toward the bust.

Red attracts all surrounding colors like a lover and displaces forms. Other colors matched to a red dress make it look bow-legged. Red roses set to one side of a bouquet weight it down.

Flowers can't help looking thin, their hips are all loins. A well-rounded woman can pass for slender if her hips slink into her loins.

In man the voice is articulated. Among animals the cry is articulated. Listen carefully to the distant crying of men's voices mixed with those of animals and you will realize that man himself is the beast.

The love-goddess types have overly voluptuous faces, each central feature slightly swollen as it rises in the trunk of the face like a turgid breast. We can hardly gaze at such breast-faces without sexual excitement, our mouthing eyes ready to lip and suck.

Making love drains our sense of smell.

No matter how well lubricated its internal and external cell structure, a plant squeaks while growing, like a motor that needs a good oiling. If our ears were attuned—as those of animals may be—to vegetable extremes of high and low pitch, who knows what cries of pleasure or pain, despair or delight, they might not pick up. Once radio microscopy develops its sonic resources far enough, we will be able to overhear the totally new world of plant talk; though decoding the messages may prove as much of a stumbling-block as interpreting the language of animals still is. If we break the code, however, it won't be thanks to science. Science depends on the cerebrum, which can disembowel the realm of matter only; unlike art, whose tool, the cerebellum, plumbs the realm of spirit. Using our racial memory we can track back along the cerebellum, by involution, to the origin of life itself. The subconscious was present at the birth of human kind, when the brain itself had hardly even been conceived. Early man didn't reason: he nosed the world like an animal. The further ahead man follows the trail of science, the more he wanders merely along the shell of the psychic universe, putting more and more distance between himself and the souls of animals, plants, flowers, and fruits—like medical science when it tries to determine a patient's real feelings by his blood density or his personality by his pulse.

Savages kiss in sudden, abrupt sallies because they are closer to instinct than we. Passion de-civilizes us, strips us to our first state: our passionate kisses are repetitive thrusts of savages.

Goodness is a civilizing force. Think of all the saints who were peasant girls to begin with and ended as *grandes dames*!

Water is a man's voice in the brook and a woman's voice in the fountain.

Shame gives us a wide-eyed look.

Adultery is a stimulant to men but a sedative to women.

Exercise develops all the muscles except those of the face which regulate the traction of the features. This is because the psychic forces controlling the face are completely unlike those that control the rest of the body and force the laws of physiology slightly out of orbit.

The nose is the only feature we have categories for. Other features are classes of one each, just like the people behind them.

In prehistoric ages time was an idea of secondary importance in life. Man was so overly occupied then that he lived immersed in the present. Boredom invented the clock and the clock increased boredom. Idleness, which banished man from the present and uncoupled him from life, gave him a sense of time as something exterior to himself, like a person on the bank watching the river flow beneath his feet. Since those distant ages when time flowed freely within us it has fled our soul and become our own jailer.

Passion cannot survive without an audience. Romeo and Juliet as castaways would have set up petty housekeeping in no time.

A woman's heart is her sex in slow motion; her sex is a thumping heart.

Dressed in fig leaves they looked more naked than ever. A flower is most naked amid its leaves. Without them it looks rather asexual.

Age adds a pane of glass each year to the lantern of the eye.

A diamond in the light is a rotating multicolored beacon, primarily blue and white. Dew on the earth at the earliest gleaming of dawn is a unidirectional beacon flashing colors intermittently, primarily yellow and white. In all natural illuminations green is accidental.

In full sunlight white serves as the reference point for all the other colors, standing in light itself, while the others try to ride the breakers in the surf of the air. The stabilizing whiteness of a woman's hips makes her almost virginal again.

White has the longest arms and shortest legs: it makes the best semaphore system. Red has the shortest arms and longest legs: it makes the fleetest messenger.

In the front of the face the features are combined in laughter by the almost indistinguishable redness of the gums and lips. Flowers being mute and their lips standing out in relief against their gums, their laughter is visually much deeper: they have no voice to complete it in aurally.

The underbrush makes the light chubby.

Petals have no "north," no cardinal points, no polarity, only back and front: which is what makes them so lively, elusive, indefinite, and infinite.

When lips smile eyes laugh. When lips laugh eyes smile.

The wind is the waves' oars, the current is the scull. The whirlpool is the water sculling in a circle.

Birdsong is always in pitch. Birds sound wrong only when frightened.

A ripple of greenery in the breeze flaring out in the opposite direction from a skimming Indian file of low cloud shadows chased by the sun. The shadows play leap-frog with the leaves, each in turn clearing the other's back. A mutual switchback railway.

What you hear in the voice of the seashell is the waves whispering in the wind's ear.

15

It's the purest bred donkey who brays loudest, thundering his stupidities.

In heartfelt prayer we kneel on our elbows as much as on our knees. In ecstasy the mouth lies prostrate in the face like a praying knee.

Red repels surrounding colors, white attracts them, yellow sets them off by themselves. Red draperies at the doorway deepen the hall behind it.

Mauve looks cold but feels warm. Red looks warm but feels cold. If you catch cold easily stay away from reds, but once you start sneezing, snuggle up to mauve.

In the sultry look of desire a woman's eyes threaten to "explode" at the whites, a man's at the pupils, and the eyes of the undersexed at the iris.

In the sunlight red burns wide, yellow flames tall. Red is the base of the pyramid of the spectrum whose apex is yellow.

Yellow is the longest lingering of colors. Yellow has the best "echo." Shut your eyes and it will be the last color to disappear.

Red has the faintest edges. When red flags billow in the wind their edges glow minutely, as if frayed. Red rags look more tattered than those of any other color.

Our eyes dust the way of their look through the smoky air, sweep the way of their look through dust.

Real jealousy never screams with anguish. More often than not jealousy is an aphrodisiac.

The sun is pure communism everywhere except in cities, where it's private property.

We can put up with our body twitching at night, but not our mind.

Goodness civilizes the intelligence.

In garnet red sleeps in blue. Garnet is hypnotic, it makes us yawn. A garnet-colored parlor lulls talk.

In mauve the sun retrieves the moon. Mauve woods on fire: sunshine and moonlight.

An animal trots with columnar hips and swivelling neck—just the opposite of man.

Half-opened petals give the flower an adenoidal look.

The eye takes good color pictures but wretched technicolor movies. It's impossible to grasp the movement of forms without letting some of the color escape.

What could be more thrilling than the depths of hell?

A look of indifference is a perpetual goodbye.

Tropical creepers are the epaulettes of nature.

Shadows adhere to red, float above yellow, sink into violet. Shadows are either inside or outside color, depending on the hue.

Too much white of the eye fattens the face.

Salt gives the taste buds a donkey ride.

All pregnant animals look hump-hipped and elbow-footed and clomp around like horses.

Grey-blue, grey-green, grey-purple, grey-black, and so forth. Grey survives in all colors except brown.

Colors are registered on the retina at different speeds of perception. If the orchestra conductor's baton were yellow, red, or green instead of black, the entire tempo of the orchestra would be different. Even the greatest musical masterpieces might have to be recomposed to fit the retina's varying perception of the different baton colors.

Our lips look less liplike when we compress them. The corners of our mouths look less like hinges when our lips are parted. The point is that if we press our lips together, the corners emerge clearly and as we open our mouths the lips are more clearly defined. Under the sway of motion the shift of balance seesaws back and forth between lips and corners so that no matter how hard we try we can never completely hide our mouths.

Straining with anger, the voice tends to break: its timbre spills over into its intonation.

In the prism white is zero longitude, yellow the equator. At noon white light reaches its highpoint, yellow light flattens out completely. Noon whitens the waterfall and gilds the river basin.

In the fiery air of noon, red burns in vermilion; vermilion flares in mauve; mauve shoots up blue flames. All blue can do is stoke the fire.

Deep red is the heaviest color of all. In a deep red dress the bust sinks to the hips, the hips to the legs.

Speech is broadcast not only from lips and nostrils but from the whole face in superfine waves that are heard not only by ears and eyes but by the whole face. The voice of the person you love sets up station-to-station broadcasting between your two faces.

Intelligent people laugh quickly and smile slowly. A slow mind lengthens the laugh and shortens the smile.

The lithe vowel rides the consonant like a horse. Vowels are jockeys: they hold their mounts on course and in check by determining the precise angle at which words leave the mouth.

Light is a limpid ball that the slightest movement ovalizes.

A grassy slope in sunlight. The grass ascends the slope when the sun is high. Everything at an angle to the light crawls toward the shade.

Banners in the wind: color riding gallop on form. Solid objects in motion: form leads color by the bridle.

Self-confidence makes a man talk, walk, and carry himself with authority. He develops a soaring glance, his neck like the stem of a flower, tall and resilient even in high winds, like a racing champion extending himself in full gallop whose neck-stem is bent with the effort but never sacrifices its elasticity or suppleness.

Color is the anvil of the sun on which the hammer of light rays keeps pounding every single second to forge and reforge form.

The wind hardens the wave which the current softens farther out, like one hand kneading paste while the other pulls it out thinly.

White has very low density. In prismatic osmosis the colors penetrate white more easily than white penetrates color. At a grand ball all the ladies are lovely until the colored dresses "dirty" the white ones. Military leaders seem to know this: they never wear white. The Pope wears it to declare his humility.

A bird's beak is a composite nose-mouth-chin. Actually, no animal face divides into three discrete parts the way a human face does—neither the nose-mouth of a dog's muzzle nor the mouth-chin of a pig's snout.

Flat green makes holes in flat yellow. Flat yellow develops hummocks in flat green. Yellow is mountainous, green is vallecular.

At the height of its trajection a waterjet puts hair rollers into the light's tresses; as the water falls back it undoes them, letting the curls tumble down.

Flowers have eye-mouth faces, the gums and the circles of the eye all of a piece.

Water leaps out of its body before throwing itself over the ledge of a falls, like a diver just before he actually dives. All naturally falling bodies fall out of themselves.

In flowers yellow flirts, white modestly withdraws. Daisies have forward eyes and chaste lips: excitement at its peak for kissing.

The Cross of Christ: transverse arm stretched out completely, upright infinitely tall. Sleep and vigil. Double symbol of death and resurrection.

Blue commas, white periods, yellow exclamation points, grey dashes, mauve colons....Mauve, the in-between color, screen divider among colors, ferryboat between color shores.

Yellow is the strongest color solvent. Yellow dissolves the other colors, even stubborn black, which it melts into brown.

A voracious sense of smell leans forward on its nostrils like a glutton eating with his elbows on the table.

Snobs use their nose to cough with.

The nose waggles its nostrils to inhale and leaps out of itself to exhale.

Dogs walk on their toes, on the forepart of the foot, using their heels as crutches. Dogs walk hobbled and hobble along briskly.

The sense of smell is the slowest of all our senses. If a piano that played odors were ever invented, one would have to finger the keys in slow motion. Moreover, there would be no purpose in executing trills on it, for the simple reason that they would never reach the nose in time.

The only sounds distance fails to amalgamate are the cries of birds. No matter how many birds are singing together their calls are interspersed with chirps. A chorus of birds practices phonetic relay races in space.

Regardless of origin, shrill noises are heard on the sides of the body, piercing noises in the back.

The current of a stream is a water pipe that moves faster than its contents.

Half-closed lashes fur the pupil. A flutter of emotion in the lashes turns the eyelids into tissue paper.

Blue, white, and red were clattering in the wind. Red clapped against white, white blushed with shame, while stolid blue merely looked on.

Light dazzle is light in greasepaint.

Light dazzle on the leaves stipples shadows over the whole plant.

The fruit pulls away from the stem's umbilical cord only when it is ripe to fall. The prematurely born infant will always be tearing away with it some of its mother's psychic integrity.

The hips step out in the clothing of their gait.

Well-being is quantitative for animals, as it is for all graceless sensualists.

There's no such thing as a caress in the round: the axes of perception would cancel each other. Proof *a priori* is the relatively imperceptible cupping caress of the eyelid on the globe of the eye.

Trees renew their leaves after each fruiting. Notice how new a woman's skin is after each childbirth.

The lips sniff at a fruity perfume while the nose drinks it in.

Clouds are wind-ribbed umbrellas.

The lips' red turns mauve with fear and orange with joy.

The nose nurses at questionable odors with its nostrils palpitating as if they were lips testing as they drink.

On the treetop the palm leaves shaken by the wind strike against each other: heel-clicking shadows on the ground.

Love: naked touch. Repulsion: gloved hands. Simple esteem: porous mittens.

Every natural object which falls by itself falls with infinitely more grace than the most graceful human body. Objects are never more awkward than when thrown by human hands.

The air is the universal microphone-loudspeaker—an ear-mouth all in one.

Regardless of the wind's direction the ship of clouds rolls but never pitches. Regardless of the wind's direction the waves make the ship pitch, themselves rolling and pitching in an identical movement. Clouds roll and pitch together only as falling raindrops in the wind's wake. Water rolls and pitches in distinct movements only in the hailstone.

Spices make the tongue fox-trot and the palate waltz. Spices are the sense of smell tap-dancing.

The whirlpool is the form of dance most like sitting down.

A trotting dog: his hind legs knit and his forelegs crochet.

The genital laziness of the mouth. The genital shallowness of the armpits.

An animal's eyes record by separate exposures, like a movie camera, while the human eye is a moving picture in itself, its film unrolling at right angles instead of merely running parallel to the image. "Seeing" in man consists of myriads of films successively entering the eye, each one a colored cell run off by the sun's rays as if they were a skein being spooled out.

The mountain ridges are the wind's dorsal spine.

The skin's complexion is a matter of texture as well as coloration. Sooner than we imagine, tints will be *woven* instead of weaves being tinted. A single blue will then have an infinite number of shades—according to the texture of the weave.

Faraway sounds come to us through hearing's keyhole, nearby sounds with the doors wide open.

The nostrils distend to inhale soft perfumes and tense up for the strong odors of spices, musk, or incense, as if to slow down their rising into the nasal passages, in order to take longer drinking them in.

Too much white of the eye enamels the teeth.

Valleys are the wind's brassiere.

To see absolute night the eye would need a sun in it and an absolute moon to see pure whiteness.

The humming voices of people in a circle; the flute-stop voices of people in a row.

Each throb of a smell that makes the nose try to leap out of its loins is like the gong beat releasing spasmodic leaps in the African's dancing haunches.

Flowers of various colors set waving by the wind: color shaking a tambourine while it dances on a leafy floor.

Breakers: water leapfrogging over the backs of waves. Sea swells: water undulating its back like a "snaked" rope.

A soft kiss sends shivers traveling to the nape of the neck. Deep kisses penetrate the skull.

Night softens the mind's irritations and inflames the body's.

Without the underbrush of salt, spices would be bare ridges in the plains of taste. Spices have no grip in unsalted food.

Salt is the police of taste. As the police protect the weak against the strong, salt keeps each of the various flavors of a course in place as much as possible and prevents them from unequal struggle, restraining the stronger from dominating the weaker. As in a well-directed orchestra the brasses often drown out the violins without "destroying" them, and the violins similarly overpower the basses; so in food salt will prevent vinegar from ruining the taste of the onions, red peppers from overcoming green pepper, and mustard from relegating ginger to the back of the palate.

The horseshoe is all heel; the tree-root is all toe. Absolute foot would be a supremely rooted plant still able to swivel.

Perfume anywhere on the skin stirs up the natural odors of the body and sends them traveling over its surface, rolling along the rails of its pores like a locomotive fired by the wind, dragging its odorous cars behind it. Perfume on the throat hollow carries the odor of the breasts into the neck; perfumed arms can be detected even as far away as the coiffure.

Dogs have less of the nomad in them than any other creature; they belong to the first race of civilized beings. See how the house dog chases off the vagrant cur with the same healthy horror his master has of any stranger without a fixed roof.

The sun is a dry launderer.

The soul's fires flicker and play on faceted pupil and beveled white of eye, flowing back and forth across the iris's plane surface like a set diamond taking its hundred free paces between the shining walls of its prison.

The flower has no weekday self, dressed as it always is in Sunday clothes.

The skin is the original perfume-pan.

The body rides upper storey in a double-boiler above the blood.

Turn blue on fast and it becomes purple. Turn purple on fast and it becomes black. Slow blue down to get grey. Slow down grey to get white. Blue is halfway between white and black: fulcrum of light, hinge of darkness.

The ideas of some men are mainly versions of their bodies, like animals of the same species.

The hypnotic result of staring fixedly at red flowers in bright sunlight is that they slip away to the right. The hypnotic result of staring fixedly at yellow flowers in bright sunlight is that they slip away to the left. A flower bed of red flowers set against a flower bed of yellow flowers in full sunlight ends in a tug of war of light.

Salivating is the mouth's sweating. Droolers perspire very little.

Water gargles with air and keeps spitting it out as saliva, but it never quite vomits until the waves press their hands along the stomach walls of the sea swell.

Green is the eraser of blue, chestnut is the washboard of green, and grey scrapes down all colors equally.

White in a painting whitens all the clean colors and sullies all the dirty ones. Any of the natural color of the canvas bleaches and soaps the picture at the same time.

Birds are the only creatures whose voices change in intonation with each change of pitch.

Yellow is the skeletal framework of the prism. Eliminate yellow from the spectrum and the structural form of light would soften and collapse and turn grey.

Rain. The water plays the harpsichord of the pond while the wind passes back and forth among the elastic strings of the falling water like Eolian hands among harpstrings.

Children's eyes see color better than form; adults' eyes see form better than color. No human eye is capable of seeing both to the same degree.

Colors are the floating markers in the ocean wastes of light, where the sun's only horizon is the human eye.

An animal's sense of time depends on whether he is famished or full. All animals react to time in the same way on an empty stomach but each according to his digestive rhythm after eating.

Light is heaviest at noon, flattening out shadows. Light *weighs* shadows down as its rays *compress* colors together.

All colors take to water in blue. A red rose on a blue dress ploughs through the weave of the material like a boat.

Flowers go in for solid colors when their petals are all of the same color and wear flowered prints when their petals are varied in color.

Absolute liquid would tremble perpetually. Absolute solid would be totally inert. In the first case the least movement would spill the liquid from its container; and in the second, by the effect of total inertia, the force of acceleration necessary to move the smallest object would so far surpass human effort that man would have to abandon his struggle for life and let himself die on the spot.

A woman's girdle is like one of those highly decorated picture-boxes of chocolates that promises so much more than it has inside.

Nose makeup doesn't exist. If any were in use it would create a gaping hole in the face.

Blue catches cold in blue-green and sneezes in grey.

We know the halls of the eye like welcome visitors but we live in our mouth.

The wrist is the leg of the hand and the neck of the arm — the extremes touching like an animal lying down with its legs in its neck. The wrist is the most "doublable" of our jointures, in terms of its length proportionately the most powerful of all known or imaginable levers.

The leaf that falls from the tree in a dead calm is an airplane steering by its tail. Leaves thrown in the wind by human hands swim through the air.

Mauve is full of shoulder movement, yellow full of hip movement. A mauve blouse worn to a yellow skirt makes the waist spiral sidewise like a cork being unscrewed.

The harsh glare that spotlights the skin partly blanks out the facial expression. The soft glow that veils the skin illuminates the face from within.

Hazy sunlight: yellow burns more hotly. Blazing sunlight: red flushes more than ever.

The wind that blows the rain around swings one of the rainbow's ends closer to the eye.

Dogs add with their front legs, subtract with their hind legs and never stop multiplying with those remarkable motors, their noses.

At the end of its golden chain the pearl seems to pour out of itself perpetually. Pearls are the sun's stalactites.

What all animals have most in common is the underbelly—winged, finned, or footed, here they are thoroughly alike. Humans, too, male or female, it makes no difference.

The cries of animals are a kind of sensory stenography in space. Early man spoke in the same way: yelping, clucking, warbling, and so forth, the way lovers still do. Instinct drags us back for a time to our prehistoric selves.

Flowers are the scented noses of plants. A bunch of flowers so sniff each other that they subtract from the total perfume of the bouquet.

As a visual phenomenon the cavity is variable in depth since color changes its capacity. Deepen a bowl by painting it blue; paint it white to make it shallow.

We would find it impossible to eat in a nauseating place. Not so with animals, whose sense of smell is on a swivel beam.

A full head of hair darkens the look of the eyes. Thick lashes smoothen the forehead.

Willfulness thickens the pupils, obstinacy thickens the whites of the eye.

Red cups out the look in one's eyes. Living in a red world would eventually make our eyes start out of their sockets.

If our eyes had to reconcile themselves indefinitely to a seagreen environment, their irises would become more transparent in color. The unmitigated murkiness of brown would work just the opposite effect, as would purple, garnet, and violet, the colors of night itself.

There are all kinds of foods we can learn to love but strange fruit makes us either shudder or surrender.

In painting, the finiteness of design keeps color below the level of the rim of form; it reaches the brim only in flowers. In the petals of flowers color is flush with design.

The hips are jointly ruled by torso and legs but resist their sway. The hips are like woman herself: seemingly submissive but actually in charge.

The nose is our most powerful facial reflex. An object coming straight at your face warns your nose first.

In moments of extreme fatigue a man no longer looks into space but lets his glance hang from the sides of the bow of his nose like the dangling legs of a rider who sits exhausted on his halted animal.

As the canvas turns elastic under the explosive force of color, so the eye expands with the percussive force of the look.

Wind overcomes water; water, granite. The grindstone has its way with steel. In the end feeling shapes thought.

The imbecile writes his look in space with painstaking penmanship so that everyone may understand what his face intended. An intelligent man's look is finely inscribed right in his own eye while it shapes vaguely symbolic linguistic characters in space as though to keep his intention to himself.

A flick of the finger nail tells whether the closed jar is empty or not. One word out of a fool's mouth is enough to convict him.

The slightest continuous breeze sets the leaves singing. The wind that runs and tumbles among the leaves sets the whole arbor twittering like children at play.

The eyes of an honest man are yoked together and in step. In the look of a hypocrite his face seems to veer this way and that as the eyes keep changing step, like two draught animals refusing to pull together.

The piano, the incisors; the brasses, the molars: the piano slices through sounds, the brasses chew them up. Now listen to the flute solo against the muted orchestral background: the symphony is eating with its front teeth.

Bronze: mauve and pink shading into each other. Bronze: equal portions of overcooked mauve and undercooked pink.

Taste is a one-room house consisting of the mouth. Hearing has the boudoir of the ear, the eyes have the parlor of the cornea, and smell has the long hall of the nose. But the poorest lodged is touch, who lives on the naked plains of the skin like a vagabond in the streets.

The humidity of the air is the wind's biceps. A slap of dry air. A wallop of wet wind.

The wave sits the current as if it were a horse, riding it relay; that is, the current changes riders every yard or so.

The body is a stairway of odors, each joint a landing.

There goes the setting sun furiously slamming the door while the moon just looks on with a half smile—one of those unusual days when mother kept father from getting his own way.

There's no fig-leaf that can cover the lips, no G-string for the mouth.

The mouth and eyes are each anagrams of the other.

Brown borders on light-colored petals make any flower look near-sighted.

The "fat" flower is more often the heavy-textured flower than the one with thick petals. It's the coarseness of the skin that makes the cheeks look so jowly.

The pores of the skin are its little ears. Scrub yourself in a hot bath and you relieve the pressure on those ears. By "turning down the volume" a good bath makes the body musical.

On questions of tasting, hearing, seeing, and touching we don't mind taking someone else's word. But only our own smelling is believing.

The swifter the top spins, the more its fat sides ovalize. A faster than fleeting look seems to come from almond-shaped eyes.

Waves clashing on the ocean's expanse swell their haunches and break out into wavelets of applause like a dancer shuddering with the drumbeat at the height of her efforts.

A crying baby trains his own hearing as well as his lungs. How many talented musicians would have been lost to the world had they not bawled so much in infancy.

Grey is the sun's ash pit.

If plants have no minds how do they decide on the amount of water their roots should draw up from the soil to staunch the thirst of their leaves? The blindly pulsating vegetable world, we say...but can a mindless plant tell how much sunlight its roots require of its leaves in the gloomy well of the subsoil?

The fur of his hide is the beast's armorial signature, while naked man has to clothe himself in a coat and a coat of arms separately.

The ordinary man's eye is a sextant useful for measuring form only. The artist's eye surveys form and color both, and by juxtaposing shades uses each as a compass to measure the other.

The mouth anchors the face. Tissue-thin lips set the face adrift.

Your nose warns you it's cold outside but can't tell one degree of warmth from another. Your chin warns you it's warm outside but can't tell one degree of cold from another.

The corners of your mouth are the first of your features to wake up in the morning and to feel drowsy at night. In other words, the corners of your mouth may be a little ahead of your lips in sensing the physical world, but they hardly come up to the cheeks, who leap out of the face's bed when you stir in the morning to resume contact with life.

The hips of light are what dazzle your eyes. The breasts of light are those twinklings you see.

The white tree trunk glimpsed in a clearing is like a sudden presence. A dark woman dressed all in white is two women.

The eye photographs idly and uses a movie camera when its interest is aroused. The soul televises at a long remove; and the heart in love telegraphs from the skin.

Hips and neck are so much of a part in woman that the hips have the neck's insolence and the neck has the hips' nonchalance.

The breasts are little hips; the mouth is an idling vagina; the arms are smaller versions of the thighs; the crotch is a greater armpit; and so on. The body is an infinite series of carnal *sandwiches* seen under an infinity of aspects.

The act of love is a mutual birth delivery between two carnal tombs in the desert cemetery of the spirit.

Copulating in love: one is unanimously and unitarily two. Copulating without love: one is alone and three.

"Ah" is the shortest as "oh" is the longest of human cries. Man is born in an "ah" and dies in an "oh," for birth is immediate and death is like an airplane taking off.

Marriage lengthens the gait of a woman's haunches and childbirth gives them a circular swing.

When famine has reduced the nose to a state of cartilage, the lobe of the ear is hardly thinner; for that drop of pendant flesh, that independent islet of the face, leads a life cut off from all the other features.

Naked feet lengthen the gait of the haunches; shoes diminish it. Naked feet undress the body to the waist. High heels have a tightening effect on the body, as if a girdle of flesh bound all its parts together.

Symbolism came into the world on the same day Adam was born, when he left the track of cause and effect to tell Eve how much he loved her, pointing out the solar disk with one sweep of his hand.

The scurrying snake sculls with his whole body—which gives him wings. The fish flopping in the grass sculls while running—which gives him legs. Rippling and rolling water flies higher in space.

Laughter is a fife-and-drum flourish.

If it didn't move so much the sun would be the finest of all precision instruments.

High heels elongate the movement of the legs toward the haunches and raise the haunches toward the torso, so that the lower part of a woman's body ends in a bird-like gait at the same time as the upper part develops an elephantine waddle. We never improve any part of the human body artificially without detracting from the natural grace of some other part.

When the body is very cold the fingers seem shorter. In extreme heat we don't even know we have palms.

Where seduction is concerned man is the better strategist, woman the superior tactician.

The lips work sounds like a potter, patting them as the fingers work clay, shaping the varying vocal cord transmissions around the flexible axis of the tongue.

Plenty of diplomats are better and more ingenious at telling lies than certain women—but there isn't one who can do it faster.

An animal wags his tail to emphasize his cries. If he had no tail his voice would strain with vehemence as a chatterbox might choke and sputter if someone tied his hands.

Like an obstetrician who relies on his instruments in a difficult delivery, the stutterer unable to cope with certain words uses the corners of his mouth as his forceps.

The movement of fire is halfway between that of air and water. A windswept flame is a flying river.

All forms and movements of things express joy: water playing on the riverbank, air wandering in the woods, the flower laughing between the patches of grass, the tree stretching itself in the sun, great clumps of furze sporting in the pond. Man comes on the scene and joy begins to deliberate and sigh. The water moves stiffly in the pipe, the air is bridled in the motor, the trimmed thicket looks rigid and dejected, the flower smiles in the vase but no longer laughs. Nature once a carefree schoolboy in the sun's playground sits down at his desk with set tasks to do.

There is no standard of good taste to surpass a flower's. A flower never wears lace in her corsage at the same time as in her gown. It's either lace petals with plain stamens or lace stamens with plain petals.

Wrist and neck are exactly alike in maneuverability. Among plants, however, the neck of the flower is usually more supple than the supplest wrist of any stem, with the possible exception of the rush, whose neck is its wrist.

The stomachs of animals are each other's graves. When a dead animal is really unwanted it means that the equilibrium of nature has been upset and that wherever a criminal outrage against her occurs the land will sooner or later be abandoned. Every country in which deaths exceed births will sooner or later be swallowed up by the jungle.

Plant roots wear thin- or thick-soled shoes according to the rugosity of the soil. The gloves worn by leaves correspond to the kind of air they flourish in. The tree clasps its bark close in winter and loosens it in summer like a man slipping his shirt tails out on a hot day.

The panic caused by fear crisscrosses the paths of the brain, confusing a person's instinctive right- or left-handedness for a sudden moment.

The animal has only one kind of memory: repetition of a thought. Animals use aphasia as a mnemonic device.

The sexual perversions are the work of oversexed minds with weak feelings or bisexual minds driven by strong feelings.

Because space is curved, light is convex as seen from the sun and concave as seen from the earth. If it were not for this domed effect, the solar rays as they ricochet against the first layers of the atmosphere would disappear into the ether, and the little light that still managed to reach us would fail to enter our eyes and glide off the pupil like a pebble skimming across the water that bounces off to land on shore. Without the curvature of space and this domed effect of light, the human eye would never catch the tiniest ray of light and we would all be blind no matter how well equipped with all the gear for trapping it.

No matter how hot or cold it is, the flower is always more moist than the leaf because the leaf breathes with its nose, the flower with its mouth.

An animal's feet are as intelligent as a man's hands.

If each letter of the alphabet were represented by a color equivalent to its sound, children would learn how to spell in half the time it takes them now.

The waves string up the water's hammocks. On stormy seas the wave-tossed boat draws less water.

The average man becomes insane when his mind gets "all mixed up." The genius goes mad when his imagination expands to the point of blotting out reason and memory, loosening their ties to reality the way a sheet of air rising too high or too quickly consumes the air around it, creating a vacuum and digging its own grave in the wild column of the vortex.

Yellow stings with lemon juice in pale yellow and stinks in brown, whose intensity increases the stench. A brown dress slows down the mild odors of the body, speeding up its strong odors: sweat, breath, and the bitter whiffs of the major joints.

The same increases in sensation apply to the taste of a fruit from pit to peel as to the smell of a rose from bud to blossom.

The light would reach us more quickly in the morning and fade more slowly at night if the whole earth were divided into vast flower beds that called forth the light at dawn and clutched it longer at nightfall. Nature instituted summer for flowers long before man took summer over for his own uses.

No receptacle can ever be united with its contents. Thinking and feeling are possible only as parallel activities, never simultaneously. They refuse to intersect each other. If they did, either the mind would catch fire from the emotions or the emotions would be held fast forever in the icy grip of the mind, and in either case the result would be death.

A drop of water parachutes down and subsides on the earth. The ovalising liquid lets itself billow out as it descends upon the tender shoots and soft hearts of young vegetable growth, which would otherwise never survive its plunging attack. The devastating force with which water strikes the hide of man and beast would wipe all plant life from the face of the earth.

What would a king be without his entourage?... With its petals fallen, the heart of the flower stops radiating.

Prophets of evil are the least mistaken, for misfortune comes headlong and good fortune from behind.

Too much talk at table fills an empty stomach and adds a course too many after dinner. Moderate conversation graces the digestion at dinner and evokes the possiblity of supper.

Animals clean themselves with the rough of the tongue, dry themselves with the flat of the tongue, and use the tip to flick with like a pocket handkerchief.

A thousand today where there was only one yesterday—but there will be as many hopes and desires tomorrow as there are tomorrows.

The seed germinates before shooting up and flowering. Doesn't the soul also take some nourishment from the corpse in the moments before resurrection?

We smell our bodies from their own depths outward, all other natural odors reach us from circumference to center. The odor of flesh is consubstantial with the sense of smell because of its carnal stronghold, the nose itself; all other natural odors come to us from outside the nose.

We ordinarily rely to some extent on our eyes to tell where a sound is coming from. In a colorless world we would be partly deaf. In a soundless world perspective would tend to flatten out. While we're asleep we hide in the corridors between the senses until a sudden awakening makes us reach for our ears to see where we are and our eyes to hearken with.

Is there any worse misfortune than to feel the body aging long before the spirit? Torture equal to the anguish of the snail who suddenly realizes how imprisoned he is in his shell.

A flowing river is an infinity of superimposed production belts.

Silence is a lawyer who pleads with his eyes.

The diamond scintillates less brilliantly with sudden than with slow, wheeling movements of the fingers. Glossy leaves throw off less light in a high wind than in a calm breeze. Sudden eye movements cast single gleams, slow movements add a thousand others.

Nothing is more certain than that war brings about greater scientific progress and more civilized amenities. Utopia may mean no more wars, but universal peace and plenty will never reign until at least one more war raises mankind to a plane of such comfort and ease that nobody on either side of a frontier can even imagine the possibility of resorting to arms. Civilization creates war and someday civilization will destroy war.

Two is civility, three is mediocrity, ten is vulgarity, and then the mob takes over, the more the uglier. The day we all become aristocrats will mean the end of aristocracy.

Men are cleverer than women at reasoning, women at drawing conclusions. Parliaments in which women were numerically superior would hasten legislation.

An anonymous crowd often intensifies our moral solitude but it has the tonic effect of making us feel more at home in our own bodies. Crowds are especially good for people who are physically dissatisfied with themselves. Women who lament the passing of their beauty should forget about cosmetics and milk baths and simply immerse themselves in crowds.

The air can do everything hands can do and rubber is just as capable as feet. Inflated tires cope with a rocky road as if they were fingers and feet picking their way through intricately.

Distance compresses the color of an object as well as the object itself. If color weren't equally affected, all far-off objects would be wearing haloes.

Lateral movements are lulling to the eyes, vertical movements awaken them. The rolling of waves induces sleep; the sight of fire keeps one awake.

Nothing is more incisive than extreme cold. As we now cut iron with an acetylene torch, some day when we shall have completely harnessed cold, tools will be unnecessary and wood will be sawed with a blade of cold.

Once upon a time opinions amounted to no more than a local disease—in those happy days when communications were so poor that intellectual plagues never exhausted their own backyards. But as soon as books began to circulate, the set opinions of any one place swarmed across the nearest frontiers everywhere and tidy little Eastern ideas headed West, passing on the way a crowd of tidy little Western ideas going East—the way the Near East and Europe exchanged diseases during the Crusades. Books are stepping stones for those who are intellectually agile but treacherous surfaces for the rest of mankind, who lose their critical footing easily and drown in a welter of ready-made ideas. Books are really useful only to people with a talent for thinking.

Smell is a one-way rectilinear sense. Hearing goes and comes towards the sound, taking roundabout routes. Sight is a fan, like water deploying in a river. Taste jogs off in all directions like an army on maneuvers. But touch is like air; it has no laws, taking its capricious way wherever pleasure prompts it to go.

Living among four walls, feeling one's glances rebound from them continually, develops eyes in the back of the head. After a long period of confinement in a room, we are for a time much more conscious than before of staring eyes at our back.

The nose is all back: the nose always looks as if it is staring into the face. It only turns round by itself when a man laughs.

Animals wake up first facially and then bodily. Men's bodies wake up before their faces do. For the animal sleeps inside his body, whereas man sleeps with his body in his mind.

The body of prehistoric man was much more adept than ours, but his mind was infinitely less capable. Modern man is more intelligent of speech than his remote ancestor, but his physical parts are oafish in comparison. Almost all primitive gestures had meanings; ours are stabs in the dark.

The forearm is the desk of the arm; the palm is the support of the wrist and in turn perches on the fingers. Each part of the arm uses the preceding part along its length as a pen for writing, a brush for painting, or a chisel for sculpturing. The arm writes, paints, or chisels in the forearm, the forearm in the wrist, the wrist in the palm, the palm in the fingers. This work-in-progress is in the form of a sketch at the shoulder and becomes progressively more finished as it inches down toward the estuary of the fingers.

The sexual act is a letter unanswered, a bottle forever adrift in the ocean. It is the only kind of one-way impact. The river never returned to its source. The only absolutely unrecapturable thrill in life.

The tip of the tongue tastes the food after serving the tongue himself, like a lackey who waits for his master to eat first.

A diamond placed too close to a pearl dims its luster like sunlight making colors fade. To prolong its life, keep your pearl next to the deep marine of an emerald.

Perhaps between twins of different sexes incest isn't really incest. Weren't they already married in their mother's womb?...

Think of all those who turn religious because they've given up all hope of enjoying life—like a woman disappointed in love taking the first man that comes along just in order to settle down for good.

In committee meetings humor is more important than ideas. The man who can make others laugh gets more votes behind a measure than a man who forces others to think.

Number is the alphabet of form, which is why children always want to touch whatever they count.

Women make us poets, children make us philosophers.

Lovemaking is a single-dish banquet for a man, but all of breakfast, lunch, dinner, and supper for a woman.

Spiders weave more webs at the time of the year when flies are swarming. Idea mongers are everywhere during periods of intellectual upheaval.

A drop of dew at dawn changes from pearl to emerald, from emerald to ruby, from ruby to sapphire and amethyst, and then goes back to pearl again, ready to begin the same color cycle once more on the carousel of sight.

A laugh held too long solidifies into the nose. The nose is the safety-valve of the face, a sort of second-degree mouth.

Just as each cell of the body contains the self in miniature, each of the features is potentially an accelerated little face. If we could speed up the look in our eyes in order to put outselves in harmony with this rhythm, the entire human body, except for the face, would be visible in every one of our features as in a flash of light. Our eye refuses to recognize these apparitions because God has definitively established the rhythm of the human look in order to put all living beings on the same plane of life. In this way every single person in the world is prevented from fleeing into his own private world and destroying the unity of social life at its roots.

Emotion washes over the cheeks in waves, pulsates in the forehead, spouts in jets on the lips, and curls round itself in the eyes.

There is nothing plump and self-satisfied about the sphere. It is neither thin nor fat but absolutely as God made it to be. The very idea that anything associated with God might be in excess is blasphemous.

The overreaching mind devours the senses and the senses too far indulged consume the mind. Philosophers end as emotional infants. Don Juan ends with the mind of a little boy.

An oncoming shower of rain sounds like a brook. The rumblings grow louder as the shower approaches, until they swell into an ocean roar as the torrents are overhead.

The butterfly swims with its legs and tail, tries to crawl with its body, and beats its wings—the threefold progress of fish, reptile, and bird all in one. Tripartite kingdom. An isosceles-triangle kind of animal.

Roses on the bush are sisters on the plant and first cousins in the vase. As one might expect, something of their common character has passed into the vase, thinning out their kinship.

The flower you pick at random in the woods is just a flower, but gather a bunch of roses and each rose becomes a little woods in itself. And the same with a woman: the more stupendous her beauty, the more she epitomizes all women. The principle of universality lies at the heart of beauty.

Suffering doesn't ennoble unless there is greatness to begin with.

Large families tend to make heredity fan out and so are more inclined to incest, a vice bound to disappear under the apartment-house conditions of modern life.

A bethrothal that lasts too long ends in a marriage of unconsummated minds.

In a small way, the eyes breathe and the mouth flutters; or, to put it differently, the eyes are a reduced version of the lungs as the mouth is a reduced version of the heart.

The females of the pack waft their odor where the males of their choice can trap the smell. Any woman with a real talent for seductive perfumery lets her scent drift upwind towards the man she cares about and downwind towards the others.

Women want to be loved sensually for their souls and spiritually in the flesh. Think of the way the lips enter the cup as the cup enters the mouth: a woman looks not only for the sensuality in sentiment but for deep caring in every embrace.

Water blindly obeys both river bed and banks. If a freshet of sufficient momentum were to swell up, it could force the stream to disobey its first masters and violate the terrain thoroughly enough to shape another bed and other banks. Water is the docile masses. The banks are the ruling classes and the river bed is the State. Revolutions change the structures of both states and their elites—periods when the people think they can be free of all restrictions. But as soon as the revolutionary torrent abates, the masses begin to realize that even if elites change and conditions improve they will still always live in subjection. Only the curb and harness have been changed.

The real criterion of intelligence is our individual capacity to define it.

Boredom complicates the masculine character and simplifies women's moods.

The cat purrs himself to sleep, being the only creature who sings his own lullaby.

We pillory those who indulge in obscene talk and enjoy looking at obscene pictures, but would anyone ever think of launching a crusade against the millions of people who enjoy breathing in obscene odors day after day? If the various religions some day discover the sinfulness of smelling and lay down the law against it as they have against all kinds of hearing, seeing, tasting, and touching, only the asexual, the undersexed, the inverts, and the impotent—those people who can't depend on their sense of smell—would obey it. Normal people foolish enough to observe the law would eventually have to give up sex.

The fingers are the sidewalks of touch and the palm is the roadway. Sensations walk on the fingers like pedestrians and drive in uninterrupted contact across the palm like automobiles.

Whether she is in the right or in the wrong, woman knows how to put man on the defensive by her onslaughts of silence. Woman knows how to keep quiet when she is in the right, whereas man under the same conditions continues talking.

Lipstick makes the lips fleshy, and by this very fact more sexual; but it deprives them of some of their natural elegance. Red crumples the petals of the lips and makes a great cherry of the mouth, destroying the bouquet in order to proffer the fruit.

Listening to talk makes us see less clearly; hearing detracts from sight. Women who enjoy being looked at know enough to keep from chattering.

The only real God is our own God. The God we pray to for ourselves is the God who is really there—unlike the doctrinal God we pray to for the sake of others. If we were as conscious of their God as we are of our own, creeds and cults would be irrelevant: human society itself would be communion enough, a kind of continuous mass.

The narcissism of our senses is the mother-lode of pleasure. Sensuality begins in the sucking of our sensory juices. We perform the act of love almost as much with ourselves as with the lover who is our non-self. Love is a masturbation of the soul.

A woman's smile betokens her psychic plenitude, which she deflates in laughter. Laughter is the exhaust pipe of her nerves; her smile is the stem winder.

Theologians reckon by eternity, philosophers in centuries, statesmen in years, politicians in days, and generals in minutes, but the seducer stands to lose everything if he isn't ready on a moment's notice.

The sweetening effect of goodness on the human face is so great that certain acts of goodness are better than a facial massage.

Physical repulsion is copulation with a third party in the room —you yourself are witness, judge, and accused. Physical repulsion in the act of love is criminal masturbation in the victimized body of a woman.

The best way to appear as if you were the most important guest is to try to look like the host.

Servants eventually come to resemble their masters. "Professional" churchgoers end up looking like priests.

Like the sun, greatness needs no proof: everybody recognizes it.

The essence of genius is to keep bumping up against folly without ever stumbling. The supreme aim of chic is to coast along the shores of ridicule constantly without once grounding.

Jewels worn on the body are like red pepper in food: they heighten the sensation of taste at the expense of the original flavor. Charm, being a compound of bodily excitations, instinctively avoids artifice.

Necessity makes gourmets of us. Luxury makes us gourmands. Women always show much more taste in choosing their undergarments than in choosing their jewels.

Tears are an aphrodisiac only at twenty.

An animal's tail responds to the signals of his various senses like an antenna reacting to wave pulsations. The tail lashes all the senses into a bundle, serving as the animal's sixth sense.

The cries of unmolested animals have neither continuity nor connection; but just break into a barnyard and fear will group the animals into a chorus around the most fearful of them as choirmaster. Collective fear has always been the secret of national unity.

Utter happiness exalts and aerates the body into a total lung, stretching deep down even into the toes.

As soon as the Devil walks the earth as an imaginary being, religion is ready to collapse.

Table talk is a form of seasoning. When the conversation wavers, the dishes seem to lack salt; when the topics are uninteresting, we instinctively reach for the pepper. A good discussion at the end of the meal makes the dessert seem cloying.

People will believe anything that mystifies them. To gain conviction, speak softly.

The wrist is the conference hall of the fingers. Before acting, the hand deliberates for a time in the fist.

All animals are experts, yet we use them merely as help. If only we knew how to get the best out of them, each in his own special capacity, we would be infinitely more successful in holding off the machines that threaten us with creeping destruction.

Good minds are never as impressed by space as mediocre minds. Walking actually conjures up greater distances then running.

A woman who knows how to carry herself can create secret openings even in the most enveloping garment. Decolletage is for women with weak sexual imaginations.

The heart is the only one of our faculties that middle-class instinct respects. The heart is either a *grand seigneur* or a nobody.

If the camellia had any smell its coldness would stand out in relief. Frigid women should stay away from perfumes.

Only liquids can be tasted by the underside of the tongue. As the bonbon begins to liquefy, the back of the tongue gradually stiffens, becoming rigid just as the chocolated-cream melts completely.

If a dancer doesn't dance inside her mind, her dancing body will never animate more than the edge of her skirt. Dancing is all or nothing.

We ward off round objects as if our hands were flat. From the distance of the soccer stadium the goalkeeper seems to be using four feet.

Laughter is the best kind of piano teacher. The height of pianistic art is to make the fingers laugh.

At the beginning of a meal the sense of taste lends capital to the sense of smell, which smell pays back with interest in the supersaturated and sickening odor that all meals have when the dinner is over.

Every artist makes the mistake of eventually wanting to turn his art into a science. Of doing what Adam did when, dissatisfied with his enjoyment of Paradise, he wanted to know "what made it tick" and how the formula was arrived at.

If we didn't talk so much about what was wrong with everything, we wouldn't be so conscious of defects. If you invoke the devil, you end up by finding him there before you.

The word God is the most perfect of all epitomes.

The more man becomes civilized the less he eats with the back of his mouth as his ancestors did. This progressive displacement of the mouth's dining room toward the front of the face is due as much to the spices which the front of the mouth enjoys as to that deplorable habit we now have of closing our mouths while we eat, thus imprisoning the tongue and preventing it from extending itself into fullest activity.

Like the kind of pastry that rises in a hot oven but deflates unless you eat it immediately, kisses you have to wait for seem to come from flat lips.

Total sexual pleasure would make us capable of tasting in *her* palate. What an impossible ideal and conclusion!

The actual color recorded by our retina reflects the slightest coloration of our moods. A painter does his best reds in moments of rage; he discovers his most beautiful blues when his mind is serene; his liveliest greens after sensual enjoyment; his most effective yellows in the darkest caves of doubt; his buoyant whites when he regains confidence; his roaring purples when maddened with pride; and the blandest of pastel shades when life is just too downright lovely.

If it weren't for the wind the air would collapse. The wind is its vertebrae, its system of disc adjustments that keep the strongest column of air from falling down. If it weren't for the vertebrae of style, ideas would collapse. Forceful expression in words stiffens the frame of thought while an idea is taking shape and then fills it out to be carried aloft like a balloon by the wind of its phrasing.

Sidelong walk, uneven shoulders, lopsided smile, one eye drooping. The old codger is listing, one half length of his frame unrelated to the other, as if preparing his body to be folded in two for the final crumpling up and disposal.

Age splits the symmetry of the face at its median line. If this cleavage occurs at the height of youth a face can look old even in full bloom.

With branches, stems, petals, flowers, and fruits it is never a question of right or left, because the plant world offers us no cardinal points of view. The only apparent direction is that every branch stands out like a right arm when we look at it and like a left arm when it looks at us. If it were otherwise, we wouldn't see space head-on as we do, but in all directions at once whenever we turned its way. If nature gave us an immediate sense of right and left whenever we looked at it, space would simply lie askew to our open eyes.

Fatigue makes us walk like the quadrupeds again, all heels and claws. An exhausted man adds the jerking of two more feet to his walk, like a lumbering throwback.

A bird's visage is caught in its own profile because the beak is so much longer than the surrounding mass of face. Seen straight on, any human face with an aquiline nose is a jumble of bird profiles.

Denial is born in the eyes. It begins to grow and then stops growing in the fixed expression of the mouth. For all final leave-takings and absolute goodbyes, "sentimentality" clamps its hold on the lips. The lips turn their back on us last of all.

Any man who acts singly in the press of a mob will get trampled. Shifting into reverse while making love can kill you.

The man of distinction reveals himself best by his "cool and collected" gestures. What we mean when we say that animals are noble beasts—that is, nobler than we—is that they never do anything superfluous.

Chins are exclusively human features, not to be found among animals. If they had chins, most animals would look like each other. After all, man was given the chin to keep the personality of his mouth and eyes from overwhelming the rest of his face, so that each individual might not become almost a species unto himself. If this were to happen, the universal ties of resemblance which make a composite race of humanity would be in danger of disappearing.

Complimentary colors side by side yearn toward each other. Put a yellow border around them and they will melt into each other. Yellow raises the emotional temperature in all color combinations.

No matter what the angle or height from which you gaze at a sheet of water, it always confronts you head-on, never alsant. Water can glance back at you any which way and yet its profile always disappears into its full face.

The movement of the waves makes us dizzy horizontally, the ship's movement makes us dizzy vertically; which is why looking at the sea makes us so sick at it.

Apes' eyes move with a bouncing restlessness. The eyes of a man trying desperately to understand something recapitulate the leap-frog look common to his animal ancestors.

Flowers are always peerlessly dressed, formal in splendor, at the height of elegance on all occasions except at the first appearance of fruit when they change into something skimpy.

The eyes of the overly fearful stammer.

All plants go bareheaded except the date palm, whose hat is so wide it hides her entire face.

The body is never asleep all of a piece at any one moment. Some of us can be sleeping soundly in our hips while our shoulders are still only dozing; others are startled at a touch on their hips but don't fully emerge from slumber until taken by the shoulders and shaken like a tree. If our bodies merely crumpled into unconsciousness instead of gliding off joint by joint, falling asleep would be a sudden drop into space while the brain looked on watching the trunk slip from under like a ripe peach. Sleeping would be more of a nightly knockout, each bedtime departure a quick death to be repeated every single day for the rest of our lives.

If there were two suns illuminating the earth instead of one, all colors would be in circumflex accent and all objects drawn up into the form of the letter "i." Color would tend to gush upward from the spout of form, and the lower part of the human body would curve inward and upward to the shoulders. Two opposing sources of light make things thinner.

Black eyes impart a blue tone to white skin. In the realm of living things, black associated with white creates blue rather than grey.

The elasticity of a form brings out its nudity. The super-supple horse in motion is animality as nudity.

Birds use their wings as a braking system, folding the porous feathers in close, stretching them out wide to balance themselves on the sharpest line of flight in a way no dancer could hope to imitate. What an airplane with porous wings might sacrifice in speed it would gain in grandeur and grace.

Imagine trying all of a sudden to freeze a waterfall: the plunging chute would jerk back up in shock, proving beyond doubt that the supposed inertness of water is a misconception: like us, it has feelings.

The oboe's humble bellow, the saxophone's goose call.... The stag bells in the trombone. Chattering castanets. The whole animal kingdom gives voice in the orchestra, all but man. All any orchestra can do is imitate the way he bawls.

Animals know how to snap at food even with their back teeth. Infants and primitives bolt food in gobbets with theirs.

Tasting, hearing, touching, seeing are all limited experiences. Smelling goes all the way, unrestrained.

The rainbow and the human face ask us to consider the same question: where does the picture begin and the frame end?

The most beautiful iris in the world relies entirely on the pupil's fire. Without the skin's warmth the most beautiful jewels in the world would gleam coldly.

We can hardly tell the difference between the beating of their wings and the sound of their voices in the buzzing of flies and bees. What about the sound of the human voice in the blowing of a brass instrument, the small voice of the breath that bursts out of its loudspeaker? The metallic voice of the brasses "talks" to us in an incredibly distorted radio blast.

Gold foams the sun's waves with silver; silver spumes mother-of-pearl over the swelling sky; mother-of-pearl crests the light with enamel. Enamel foams as zinc, zinc as tin, tin as lead. Metals are the luminous detritus of each other.

The youthful movements of the little finger rarely decrease, even with extreme age; for the little finger is guided by intuition, and like charm intuition never changes.

If we could talk audibly to ourselves from within, not in sudden, unpredictable hallucinations but systematically and continuously, we should be so self-sufficient that we would willingly remain mute forever. Nothing enchants man so much as hearing the sound of his own voice. Trappists and yogis know this sensual gratification so well that when they are forced to hear other men's voices the sound seems to come from hell. Silence puts us into the paradise of ourselves.

Spices wound our sense of taste; salt dresses the wound. Spices without salt make the mouth salivate after the feast is over like a wound that wells up with blood.

Death is the bowel movement of the soul evacuating the body by intense pressure on the spiritual anus.

Dust flies, yet it has no wings. If we could blow up our bodies with Mind, we would float in the air like dust particles. The wings of angels are nothing but symbols of their ideal nature: their tremendous psychic opulence. Christ walked on the water as in a psychic balloon. Had he thrown himself into space at the Tempter's behest he would have floated to earth like a parachutist. One might say that a person's real weight can be determined only when his mood is normal. Anger adds pounds; serenity helps you reduce.

The air kisses the water with pursed lips. The water kisses the air with the corner of its mouth. Only we living beings kiss mouth to mouth.

In order to appreciate the sensibility of the chin look at the face upside down. For then, like an hour-glass reversed, the sensibility of the lips, which a moment before completely inundated the chin, flows back into the lips, liberating the chin's hidden psychic force and reinvesting it with personality.

A moody silence between lovers is a shared widowhood.

A ravenous fire smacks its tongue and licks its chops with exactly the same gesture as all other natural forms. There are hundreds of ways of using teeth and lips for eating but in the entire living world only one way to eat with the tongue.

We can see two objects at the same time but not two faces at the same time, because the human face is a whole, whereas any and every object is never more than a particle of some entirety. Only the human face can milk our glance dry.

When we look lovingly, out peripheral vision goes blind. The saint's halo isn't so much a part of the saint himself as a dazzling overflow at the edge of our absolute visual absorption in his uniqueness.

Touch is the rope and fastener of the necklace of the senses.

Animals have no sense of shame except—incredibly enough—for the shame of drinking. Witness the peculiar contortions they go through at the water hole, the curious way they turn their heads to one side as if wanting to apologize.

Tie the sleepwalker to his bed and he takes off in spirit. Many phantoms aren't the spectres we suppose but much more likely doubles of sleepwalkers who happen to be too sick to leave their beds, and since they can't leave they send their psychic selves.

Back to front the shoulder is more or less the same. If this part of the body weren't even as relatively stable as it is, the body in the act of walking would seem to be endlessly revolving.

The pupil contributes its weight, the white its volume, the iris its solidity to the power of the glance.

God has to enlarge the boundaries of Paradise to admit every middle-class soul who wants to enter, otherwise the non-middle-class residents would be asphyxiated. The middle-class atmosphere diminishes.

The air is all forearm and wields a long slap.

Pleasure as it increases contracts itself little by little on the skin, ending in needle pricks. Pain is a spreading oil stain.

Water changes timbre with its angle of impact and intonation with its volume.

Objects are the clasps on the pockets of space.

The look of the eye functions according to the sun's force of gravity as well as the earth's. Without the combination of the two it would either plummet down as soon as it left the eye or soar into the sky of the forehead.

The right hand is more gifted with lateral movement and the left hand with vertical movement, so that the arms as they combine gestures are equilibrated. The dancer unable to divorce her arms in the dance would always seem to swim as she danced, like a fish lumbering about on the surface of the water.

The wind adds a palm to the rain's fingers. The slap of a gust of wind is incomplete unless mixed with rain.

Men think more in terms of length, women more in terms of breadth. Walking straight ahead, a man is less likely to trip and fall, even as a woman circling around the cocktail party is less likely to jostle others.

The Burning Bush is a proto-symbol of the Crucifixion. Had Christ not been "on another plane" at the time of his crucifixion, his own body would have set the cross on fire.

Immediately before it falls, water turns into a living being, as if a personal soul had just slipped into it: look at the way it twists and turns, writhing in desperation. (What if you threw a not quite cold corpse out of an airplane—would the dead awaken?...)

Women use the smile as a cutting arm, the laugh as a firearm, and the smile and laugh together as a pair of ripping claws.

The path of greatness is a one-way street. Let the traveler try to reverse direction and either he changes into a salt pillar like Lot's wife or gets trampled underfoot by the mob, since all human-kind is already hot on his heels.

If the upper part of the face were not contained by the eyebrows, the forehead would sink down into the eyes while they floated up towards it. The upper face would heave about in all directions with its expression in a continual tidal wave.

A bird puffs out its wings to make shrill cries. Every singer has broad shoulders while hitting loud notes.

Sunlight transforms the spider's web into a golden net and the spider into a carbuncle. Even in deepest hell the wicked are enveloped in God's love, which at least keeps their ugliness hidden from each other.

You can never arrive at the end of the world on a planet. The human face has no end point either, because of its spherical expression.

At a distance human movements take on an animal character even as those of animals look human. There's nothing like seeing from afar moving shadow-pictures of men and beasts together to make you realize how closely related are animal kingdom and human species.

A charming woman channels her smiling but fans out her laughter.

A scarlet bow would make a mass of jet-black hair gleam with blue diamonds.

Barking is canine back-fence chatter. When dogs have something they really want to say, they growl.

The eye offers retail looks at the soul's merchandise that the mouth expresses in bulk lots.

The sheer transparency of light at the end of the tunnel reminds us of how much the brightness of the eye owes to the blackness of the pupil.

A horse racing at top speed tends to rip its own saddle off, throwing the rider violently backward. When the sun rides two clouds at once it slides back towards a croup, making the underbrush rise up towards one croup of the mountain and the grass tumble down on the other side.

When fatigue, discouragement, or fright creases the look, the pupil folds in on itself vertically and the iris horizontally. The eye would seem to have been crucified.

The features of the face comprise an archipelago threaded by a thousand narrows but no isthmus. If the features had just one, the whole face would keep revolving like a carousel.

The leaf may be yellow, green, red, purple, or white, but it never has blue veins. If it had, it would seem to exist in a permanent state of laughter.

The human eye has no vestibule, peristyle, forecourt, antechamber, etc. The eye lives in the street. A man can be a king, prince, or beggar, but when he looks at you his eyes come right out and rub elbows democratically as in a packed crowd.

God is unidirectional, which is why there's no returning from the other world, or from after to before. You can't "turn back" from God. The road to Hell is not in the opposite direction from God's road but at right angles to it, so that, in effect, God acts as a structural brace between the two, seeing to it that Hell doesn't flow into Heaven.

All the features of the face are inward-tending—psychic tunnels leading into the abyss of the soul. Only the cheeks have outer walls. Blushing posts placards about feelings.

Good taste has no fixed rules, though fashion has. Taste amounts to being fashionable with a sense of style.

The love of God is the height of sentimental ecstasy. The depths are found in married love, whose chain of affectionate caresses leads to the sub-foundation of the building, where sexuality reigns supreme. No matter how much he tries, the completely asexual devotee of the Lord will never learn to love Him.

As the bird grows, all the parts of its body retain their relative proportions more strictly than those of any other animal. Even its wingspread follows its body weight like an obedient compass leg. Creeping creatures like snails, caterpillars, and snakes were originally perhaps airborne, whose wings for some mysterious reason failed to adapt in growth to the rhythmical increase in the body as a whole, and in the course of time folded themselves more and more about their frames, eventually becoming integral body parts. As this happened the animal gradually lost altitude, lowering its flight to a mere glide above its own shadow until all it could do was jump along in jerks. And at last it clung to the earth and never again left it. The evolution of caterpillar to butterfly via the chrysalid is no doubt a devolutionary reaction to this early development. Since everything in nature is cyclical, surely one day, by inverse reaction, what we call birds today will end up flush to the ground while caterpillars, snakes, and snails will return aloft as before.

When animals act pleased with themselves they wag their tails to show it. They confront the world with their own superiority by holding their heads erect. The human race being tailless, we show how vain we are by swaggering.

The rainbow can never become part of the sun again. If manifestations of divinity were resumed by God again they would smother Him. Only the Son can return to the Father because he is consubstantial with His essence.

The thirsty animal drinks with his teeth, crazed with the desire to eat water. Man, too, sees his shrivelled lips turn to dust with the longing for water.

Break one of the panes in a rose window and it ceases to revolve. Cheeks whose fullness is shattered become merely a slice of flesh, losing their expression.

If we shipped off all the animals in another Ark, leaving all but a single species of turkey cock or ape or horse—that unique remainder would perish in a short while by simple degeneration, and the last remnants would branch out again by force of evolution into divergent types, straining to distinguish themselves from the parental stump. They would develop into new animals in order to counterbalance the stifling unity created by a predominant single race. So, nature would regain its equilibrium. The same would be true of plants: monoculture ends up in new varieties. Nor would humans be any different. Do we not see the union of first cousins give rise to completely new types stranger to the race, spiritual and even physical bastards of the others? Nature will never be tamed or caged.

Hold a ruby against a pearl and from the distance the ruby seems to circle the pearl with a fiery ring about its iridescence. Heaps of pearls and rubies dance around each other in the light with mingled twists and turns.

Noon is the fattening time of walls, making them wider. Afternoon adds to their height. The sun creates cyclical changes in the human form during its daily round from East to West, bathing it in the world of appearance.

The upper lip follows the dictates of the right eye. The lower lip similarly obeys the left eye, leaving just enough room between the union of their gestures to let the other features filter through their play of expression. In the concert hall, orchestra and choir seep through the soloists.

The brilliance of sunshine is a rapid tattoo of slaps. Blinding light on water is like a "rabbit punch." There is something shameful about being dazzled: even persons of remarkable sensibility feel a vague inclination to blush then.

The eye is the most elastic kind of compass and refuses to be stabilized except when it reckons by square measure.

We sometimes laugh ear to ear; but it would be impossible to smile wider than the distance between our two eyes.

Our hearing tries to measure the depth of sound when we are in good health. Once ill, we are interested only in the length of sounds.

If the imaginative shifts of the mind did not drag something like memory in their wake, new ideas, once recognized, could never be grasped long enough to be safely stored away. Although this mnesic trailer that travels along behind partakes of the nature of both memory and imagination, it still lacks a name: hardly anyone suspects its existence, let alone its function. This is the faculty that hauls dreams up into reality. It represents the distinguishing suture between cerebrum and cerebellum. Without it we would never be able to remember the night's dreams. Without it our deepest sources of inspiration would wash out over everything as soon as we perceived them. Thanks to it man can return from his descent into ecstasy—he need not dangle over dream and trance forever. What we usually mean by madness is the effect of finding the road blocked on the way back.

Imagine how many priests there must be who are poets but haven't yet found the lyre they've been looking for. And just think of how many poets there are who in all other respects are actually priests without knowing it.

At her orgastic peak a woman suddenly dimples all over like a pomegranate that, ripening, bursts.

When nose and palate are at odds about a dish, tongue keeps to the sidelines. When a foul-smelling dish tickles the palate, the tongue impassively spoons it up out of duty alone. When it so happens that nose and palate wholeheartedly agree, the tongue salivates freely and enjoys the dish to the full as if to purloin the greedy palate's portion.

Shadows round everything out. The lacework of light is based on a circular pattern.

Yellow and blue can't control themselves from blending together as green. Adjacent in fabrics, they slide off into each other. A yellow bodice on a blue dress slips below like underwear while the blue climbs over it, stretching the wearer's waist towards her bust. Unless it has a touch of indigo in it, blue simply soaks up any yellow that gets too close.

All in all, the laws represent a minority plot against the best interests of the majority, which is why there are always more policemen patrolling the other side of the railroad tracks than the center of town.

There is no distinction between lying and stealing. Nobody has ever told a lie that wasn't essentially, no matter how you look at it, a veiled attempt to appropriate a sackful of someone else's moral possessions through forcible entry.

Women are sentimental heroes and intellectual cowards. The woman who would kill herself for a man would also betray an idea without thinking twice.

Death is easier to define than life, minus being much more exact than plus.

What goes on in an animal's mind when he comes upon the corpse of another animal? Do animals have the same idea of death as we do: the atheist's certainty of total dissolution, the true believer's confidence in his journey to another world? Maybe they simply believe in the transmigration of souls and that the body's death has no meaning since the living soul is already being reborn in the flesh and blood of a new creature?...But whatever it is that animals really think makes no difference when you consider that they all live at high noon—and who thinks of dying then? In that respect all animals are as unconcerned about death as Renaissance princes.

Nothing makes you want to dance as much as the wind, best of all dancing masters, surpassed only by flowing water with its hip movement.

The pylon is the highest of all crosses, the arms of the cross no longer extended for blessing but folded into the torso for praying.

Aren't Egyptian obelisks all but crosses already, the first pre-Christian symbols of prayer for the advent of the Messiah, symbolic John the Baptists announcing the symbolic Cross?

Notice how animals behave in the smoke of fire. Where men react simply with wounded eyes, animals seem to enjoy the torture of it—as if pleasure and pain together comprised a separate sense. Hardly any animal makes love without a certain masochistic gratification. If the cock isn't tortured by the hen's flight before he thrusts himself into her, if she herself isn't ultimately attacked and overpowered, neither can enjoy coitus.

The wind not only renews the air but puts new light into it since all air is saturated with light. On sunless days look to the wind.

Concave objects are the wind's prompting boxes. What beautiful delivery when the wind blows above a hole in the ground!

The nose is the landing field for all grimaces.

In mixed company women practice a kind of visual stenography which they slowly and painstakingly decode later among other women.

The human body is the most precious of perfume bottles, but unlike ordinary containers which must be opened, it does not yield all its odor unless pressed. Pressure forces out the personal fragrance of the human body.

The first streak of dawn creates twilight in the west.

An early morning moon tints the pale blue of the sky with opal. A dying moon washes the sky pinkly with its blood.

Sunlight lends a halo to reds and tends even more to inflate yellows. Yellow flowers seen at the fine point of noon are balloons bobbing on their string-stems, filled with the urge to fly free.

There is an intimate connection between tongue and lips in man. In animals each of those features is under separate orders. The proof may be seen in man's ability to spit: all an animal can do is salivate.

The circling of the air through valleys is the oldest of all waltzes. The wind fox trots on the mountain passes. Headlong gusts polka from the clouded sky. The wind has always been "up" on the latest dance.

In summer our joints ventilate our limbs through the powerful unremitting process of sweating. When winter comes they bank their fires: a central heating system for the great bare floors of the skin.

Flowers all bloom like a knotted silk handkerchief easing open and then shaking loose—all but the budding rose, which fans out from the center, spurting up in a *V* like a pocket handkerchief.

Any object's opening is its eye. The sphere, being smooth all over—all back and no front like God Himself, whose eye we never see—is pure narcissism, all the parts of its body drawn up out of sight, fronting its inward stare.

The neck is the supplest of all elastic joints and can move by itself on three planes. Rubber is the only thing like it. If not for its elasticity, our heads would have wooden or waxen faces like those of people suffering from stiff necks who are incapable of "outward glances" and because of this paralysis of the neck seem to do all their smiling, laughing, etc., inside their faces.

In the throes of desire the pupils of a man's eyes and the whites of a woman's eyes protrude.

The smile is all postscript, the laugh all preface. The smile matures fully just before it dies, the laugh dies incognito. This is why trying to decipher a woman's laugh or smile is so frustrating: her smiling is always being interrupted by stifled laughs, and even her laughter is occasionally intercalated by smiles.

A man's sex is a passageway between his thought and feeling, and he rarely stays there any length of time. A woman turns the same passageway into bedroom, boudoir, and dining room, the rest of her body being merely a showplace resplendent with carpeting, indirect lighting, and conversation pieces. A man wanders through his sex to discover what it is he really feels. A woman simply lives there, her sex being her castle, the only seat of her sensibility. Old maids are such hard-hearted creatures because they are always desperately trying to fly their sensual home grounds.

A fountain of water is all ball-bearings, so perfect in function that it requires no lubrication. Water is the only substance friction will not wear out.

In blurring color at a distance speed is the prototype of camouflage. If the eyes never moved they would see everything through a grating.

Cemeteries are the souvenir albums of Time deified. After many decades have passed, once the graveyard becomes historical, it begins to resemble a mania that persists beyond the reason for its psychological purpose, or one of those tics that outlasts the disease it was supposed to pacify.

The skin opens or closes the calyx of its odors according to the body's heat, psychological state, or position. By comparison, a single hair is a flask of perfume with the stopper removed all hours of day and night.

The front teeth guillotine food. The incisors put it to the sword. The molars massacre the survivors like waiting thugs. Nothing looks more vulgar than eating with the back teeth only.

No tic is more concentrated than the nose grimace, which pulls on all the features at once, disintegrating the whole facial expression from its golden center to its outer limits. No wonder the insane are so prone to nose tics.

There's no preferential treatment in Nature: necessity directs priority.

A man uses his fingers more than a child, who depends on his palm. These are, respectively, the carpentry and masonry of gesture.

In man the call of appetite is rarely heard from farther down than the stomach. Animals feel it even in the intestines, an entrail-hunger humans know only in times of famine or after long fasting.

By day the nose is an adaptable arras which at noon sets up a kiosk of shade in the face as if to protect the burning lips from the sun's furnace. Photographed at high noon the face looks as if it were under a tent.

When the nacreous clot of the white of the eye begins to run, its enamel pearls with desire. Selfishness turns it into bone and greed into a shimmering tin. Out of the crucible of the human eye, the universal symbol of all living forms, comes every imaginable transmutation.

Artists are only students of light apprenticed to flowers as their only teacher. Artists practice the art of coloring under flowers who teach the science of color, an intuitive and absolute science that makes the slightest deflection in taste or judgment impossible. There is no greater master of color or form than the flower, and she teaches by looking: not you looking at her but her looking at you. The real painter is the one who lets the flower hold him in her gaze, not the celebrated artist with his priceless work.

As the sun goes down the moon grows brighter. The lights and darks that film the pupil's brilliance toward nightfall make the white of the eye gleam with silver.

Our senses have become so dulled since prehistoric times that without spices to stimulate their appetite, the lips of most men would no longer do more than serve up food to the mouth. The lips are now so insensitive that they have abbreviated our sense of taste: it takes us twice as long to "test the tastiness" of food as it took our savage ancestors. Our partially paralyzed lips slow down the salivation rate so that our glands learn to expect the flick of the spice's whip in order to keep going. So many prophets predict the end of the human race through physical cataclysm or moral upheaval—isn't the doom of our species equally imaginable as the result of progressive degeneration in our sense of taste, the pivotal sense of life, which has made it more and more difficult for us to assimilate food? Our sensory debilitation may even continue to the point of disabling us from meeting the physical demands of survival on this planet.

Woman steers among the reefs of man by using her eyes as sextant, her sex as compass, and her mouth as rudder.

Fire looks like an inflamed eyelid when seen too close. The eye of fire looks more real at a distance and sees best from afar. Out of the fantastic remoteness of its telescopic eye the star looks at us almost as if its glance were human.

The mass repeats on a divine plane the same rhythmical progression as the act of love on the human plane. The carnal immolation of coition and the spiritual immolation of the Crucifixion are agonies connected on two levels—two agonies but the same mass, each an infinite extension of the other.

The fingers need to be educated. The thumb is born knowledgeable. Children have assurance ingrained in their thumbs, babies as well as boys; for the thumb is all instinct and wakes up to life in a flash at birth. The thumb trembling in the hand of a dying man announces the departure of his soul.

He from whom the Eucharist derived being himself the Eucharist, unleavened bread could have no meaning for him. The only form of divine communion possible for him was autoconsumption—or, to put it differently, to make his carnal nature progressively disappear as he sublimated it in the Divine. Christ suffered so greatly because he partook of himself in a supreme act of self-despoliation in order to perfect his essence and make everything divine in his own self. The same principle obtains in any man who achieves regeneration through stripping himself bare, except that in man the process is cerebral only, whereas Christ's was the total despoliation of his entire being transecting all the planes of his humanity. Christ's crucifixion endured thirty long years, the cross being merely the ultimate nail that expelled the remains of his human nature.

Why do thinkers rack their brains trying to understand how sensations can become thoughts? All philosophical solutions err in docketing and ticketing our faculties and their forms of expression like a butcher calculating joints or a librarian cataloguing tomes. *The mind is a unity.* Idea and sensation are involutions of each other, inside and outside of a single glove belonging to the same hand. Notice how the thought that affrights our mind forces out of us the same cry of pain that rips our flesh.

Good taste is a matter of choice; style, a reflex action.

A water spout is a first-class erection, a liquid pistil in the well of the flower, a wet snowing of pollen. The water spouting into the basin drones its fecundity into barren wastes.

Only man knows what it means to be in the springtime of ideas, whereas woman is in eternal summer. They respectively symbolize the creative spirit of repetitive growth, and the intuitive vase of receptivity endlessly open to life's universal message—like an omnidirectional radio receiver.

By means of a system of "artificial clouds" along the lines of a mirage, we shall one day elevate whole cities into space in successive relays on the white canvas of the cloud piles, making natural movies in open daylight—a kind of first-degree TV.

The look of the eye is a ruler racing on paper, a wandering compass, and a restless set-square.

Artless innocence has its nose in the wind like a ship bereft of its tiller, skidding through the waves.

A beautiful female body is the best kind of bed lamp. Sleeping side by side makes the night less opaque.

The shortest straight line never becomes a point because the point has no length. From end to end the point encompasses the distance between the image that enters the eye and the look that leaves it.

Breasts restrained by a brassiere are like two tennis balls expelled by the rib cage that fall back into the net at each stroke.

No flower in existence—whether streaked or smooth, long and slender or wide and squat, bony or fleshy, with stamen reaching only to the bottom of its petals or extending proud moustaches into its face—no flower wears a chin beard except the orchid, whose petals overflow into its face like a river of white whiskers. This accounts for the orchid's weary grace, for its antiquated and antediluvian look. Orchids are outmoded, like heirloom furniture in a modern living room; set beside "modern" roses they throw the charm of the bouquet out of joint. The ancient air of orchids emanates from the night of time in which our own racial memory is so completely lost that the orchid seems transplanted from an infinitely older planet than the one we inhabit.

Nobody exercises his sense of critical justice against himself. Nobody sees himself as he is. Nevertheless, even the least little nobody preserves an *unconscious* critical spirit whose wheels turn on their own to keep his personal autonomy, individuality, and indivisibility functioning so that he can never live anyone else's life but his own—never exist as that other person he thinks he is. There, ultimately, is where self-love originates. Self-love is the sharp-eyed creature inside your skin who can read between the lines, who tells you *unconsciously* that you are what your neighbor thinks you are, not what you believe yourself to be—at the same time as you refuse to accept the verdict with your conscious mind. And so self-love cries out and rebels. Almost all the violence and rancour in the world comes from the desperations of self-love.

Death is electrocution from a vital charge sparked from the great beyond: this world's voltage would be too weak. Put all humanity end to end in electrical continuity and you still wouldn't produce a millionth of the electro-psychical force equal to the weakest discharge of all the angels in Paradise.

The final test of beauty is that it remain beautiful in ugly surroundings. Whenever the frame affects the beauty of a painting it is always a sign that to some extent the painting deserves its frame.

The entire personality of the hand lies in the thumb and forefinger. Amputate all the other fingers and in essence the hand will still continue to exist. But amputate thumb and forefinger, and the others become vibrating pincers; for only the forefinger can take initiative, only the thumb assume responsibility. The ring finger, the middle finger, and the little one are good workers, always ready and busy, never shirking a job—but they can never rise above the position of foreman, no matter what they do.

Nothing is so sensitive to concavity as the tongue, so used to its own lair that it conceives of all other resting places in like form. Tasting is ideally convex but in practice the dishes one eats pull tasting out of shape. At rest the tongue lies in the housing of the mouth as if it were safe in a cylindrical cabinet.

The act of love undoes our carnality in a small-scale resurrection. Death may be a spasm extending into the other world in the same way a newborn baby's first cry is connected with the cry of a lover in orgasm.

An animal's teeth are all "wisdom" teeth: you never find an animal pitting or gritting their hardness against anything more resistant than a bone. An animal's teeth are endowed with foreknowledge, for apart from his brains, an animal's body is all instinct. He actually sees with his teeth.

In the animal kingdom the longer the tail, the wilier the species. The tail reaches its greatest length in the snake, which is all tail. When humans had tails those of women must have been longer, since they are wilier than men; and they probably showed their tails to everyone without waiting to be asked, just as they proudly show off their hair now. Since the tongue is associated with the tail in all living beings, women keep busy wagging their tongues because they no longer have any tails to wag. What they need to keep from chattering is a moral tail: clothes, children, domesticity, sentimental or sexual pursuits. Nothing keeps a woman's tongue so still as the inexpressible pleasure of her hips quivering in a new dress—a reflex gesture common to the first Eves, who used to whip the air in frenzy with their tails at each thrill of delight in Eden.

Entering a church one peels off the social self, which is left outside like an overcoat in the cloakroom to be put on again upon leaving. When the mass is over you can read a pompous *whew!* on every face—like the look on the face of a man who has just found something he had lost.

If churches were coffin shaped, believers would shun them like the plague. We take drugs to forget life and go to church to forget death.

Animals have no sense of progress or purpose, they have nothing to look forward to because their aims are what they already are. No matter how much their adroit movements express their thirst for life, lack of imagination keeps them mentally unruffled. The stupid beast has made it to the top as we never can.

The Devil is the fourth dimension of churches.

We feel like fully resident landlords in the upper part of our body but merely like tenants of the rest. We feel our shoulders as parts of ourselves, our hips as belonging to someone else. When we walk our shoulders swing freely while the movement of our hips *seems to come* from another self that now and then doesn't even seem to be remotely like us. But once we throw ourselves unreservedly into any kind of dancing the whole motion *stems* independently from our hips as if they were a second brain.

Back-flows shape the water into faces. Features keep swirling up loosely like the sections of a simpleton's face.

Religions come and go, the idea of God occupies people's minds and then disappears, but the idea of the Devil is an instinct and persists. We adore God in flashes, our fears never leave us.

After a certain point the idea of spaciousness makes you think of length. Our strongest sense of spaciousness as width is the distance between our own eyes which eventually verges on infinity. It looks as if the hypnotist's feat, ultimately, consists of forcing our eyes apart with his single glance until they spread out interminably. The effect is that sudden drop before sleep takes over.

In the true poet the cerebrum is a lyre played by the cerebellum.

An animal's upturned tail means that his hat is on—it's like a feather stuck upright on the back of his head. Quadrupeds are never so naked-seeming as when their tails hang low.

God is everywhere in nature, but wherever you look for him he travels incognito. What keeps us from identifying him is that our minds are complicated whereas God is simple.

God is twice-God for woman because she sees him through man, which is why in women religious feeling tends to be "pushy."

At the same time, what prevents women from making good priests is precisely that even at the altar they confuse the cult of man with the cult of God. Having originated in Adam's rib, they can hardly expect to escape this dilemma. Old maids get their sanctimonious airs from fanatic adoration of the man they can't find in the God they already have close at hand.

The haunches are a foolproof concentration camp. We have some leeway in our shoulders, our legs, our necks, our torsos, and so forth, but we are prisoners of our haunches. Only dancing gives us an illusion of detachment from the confines of that "organ." Only the act of love can free us completely.

Laughter is the best hepatic antitoxin. A happy drunk can make one glass do for two.

A measure of seriousness in their laughter is the distinctive mark of great spirits and beautiful souls—the rarest type of humanity. Broadly speaking, people are of two sorts: the glum ones and those who guffaw over trifles. Unforced laughter is perhaps the surest psychological gauge of greatness of character, if we judge by the perfect standards of laughter in the world of nature: the serious tones of the river are interspersed with proportionate peals of laughter, the gleeful whispering of the wind in the branches has its sober, confidential side, and the rain's tears tinkle. All nature testifies to the same just mixture of temperamental attributes. It was the Fall that brought the laugh so low. The decline of true laughter is the result of raw nerves exhausted by the pressures of modern life. We have degenerated to the vulgar level of snorting and snickering.

No plant steals from its neighbor more sunlight than its own vitality requires. A tree that grows taller than normal grows thinner than normal.

The white of the eye differs from all other parts of the body in kind, quality, and texture. The pupil reflects us completely but even the white of the eye has a little something to say about the world in which it participates, its fluid mixtures always pick up a few traces of the light that reflects us just as a glass whose bottom has been plated can be used as a mirror.

Man began life on all fours. He has since straightened up—apart from those of his slightly hunched-over, sunken-necked primitive cousins still on earth. The end of the human race will undoubtedly be marked by the chest's retreating toward the back and by the loins hollowing out, like an aging tree coiling in on itself. Bent in two at his inception, man will look split in two at his end. Living specimens with receding busts scooped out of their backs tell us even now that sooner or later the family of man, a whole race known under its own name, will come to an end.

Hypocrisy puts the eyes at a crossroad.

Some human voices are impressively so much more than human that they seem to have come directly from Paradise. Their sound leaves the brain by way of the spinal column like a wire walker traveling the length of his track and reverberating softly on that super-sensory trampoline, the coccyx, the final echo chamber of sound, as each exquisite pulsation rises and rebounds toward the mind the way an athlete springs from the trampoline's shelf to spray himself into space again.

The neck contains all the body's articulations, those of the fingers, wrists, knees, toes, shoulder and ankle joints, including the majestic back itself, with its infinite pliancies of movement—all the body's articulations in one, a synthesis of syntheses of every rhythmic movement of the body. If the neck did not transmit this complete repertory of gestures to the head there would never be any connection between the head's bearing and the body's progress, and a walking man would look as if he were splitting himself in two with each pulsation forward. Head and body would go leaping out and at each other like the contents of a wagon bounding crazily against the differing rhythm of its carriage. The best example of the way in which the neck is married to the rest of the body, unifying the human walk from head to toe, is the bamboo, whose head and body belong to each other in their complete agreement as a total neck.

The whole body breathes, not only the lungs. Every body cell palpitates, not only the heart. The whole body sees and not just the eyes. The whole body hears and not just the ears. The human body is a total touching machine, one of the brain's principal functions being to serve as a sensory mirror in which the soul, like a bewildered Narcissus, manages to contemplate its own image.

The act of love is all our senses bunching around the stem of time.

The hurricane's whip strains and pulls out the branches of trees until the entire forest bristles with arms. A terror-stricken crowd looks like a dishevelled mass of arms.

The rays of sunlight that ordinarily stipple color finally get to use a flat brush technique in the rainbow.

Yellow is the common denominator of color.

Tormented by the wind the branch tenses and strains like a human arm. Terror turns a man's arm into a hanging stalk. Extreme suffering upsets the balance of nature.

Pregnant women are prone to longings. All born creators develop uncontrolled cravings as if they were trying desperately to cling to reality the more their creative imaginations soared.

The act of love is an overlapping ebb and flow, like two streams brushing past each other in opposite directions. How else explain the way in which the act of love strips us down, makes us feel disembodied, twice naked, totally naked?

If instead of exploding in the empty, invisible space beyond the natural world the act of love took place totally in nature, its superconcentration of vitality would easily surpass the force of ten thousand atomic bombs.

The river doesn't deposit its gradually accumulating detritus with design, rather it loosens it like phlegm from obtrusive angles along its throaty passage. So also the *idée fixe*, which uses everything in its path as an excuse to ball up and dam up the mind.

Light has much more talent for broad coloring than fine sketching except in the crystalloids, diamonds, and snowflakes, all of which are really miniature suns in themselves. The sun doesn't draw very well but paints divinely.

The wing of a bird is a soundless skate, silken rollers traversing cotton wool, two palms brushing. The wing of a bird is a soaring caress, a kiss on wings.

The act of love is the shortest form of forgetfulness. If it were really possible to make it last longer, women would become drugs.

Man, making love, uncreates himself, returns to all-encompassing nature's womb. The sexual act is a "degeneration" on the road to infinity, inverting death, reversing birth, annihilating time and space. The sexual act may be the first stage of afterlife, the ground floor of the world of spirit.

A head of hair is a frameless hat. If hair had restrictions all hats would look placed alike no matter where or how stuck on. In other words: the hat does nothing for the coiffure, the coiffure does everything for the hat. All hats are becoming to their hair environment.

Our eyes can never get *divorced* because their look is one and indivisible. On the other hand, nothing is easier than to have our lips going each its own way: one bristling with irony, the other simple and submissive; one gay, the other sad; one baleful, the other placating; one beckoning, the other rebuffing. The lips are the most perfect jewel case for the divided ego. The look of our eyes may be all of a piece, but those two lips of ours clamp themselves so closely on our wriggling selves that we can free only one inch of ourselves at a time. Of all our split instincts the mouth plays Hamlet best. What draws us to the Mona Lisa's mouth is that its thousands of lips never achieve even the fraction of a mouth, their multiplicity always short of making one thing alone, jig-sawn pieces of an uncompleted puzzle. Mysteriously Mona Lisa smiles on with something of the mystery of all women.

At some point all sensations begin to mean more than they say, and turn into codes and languages—all except smells, whose statements are transparent. It is impossible for a smell to get its message-direction wrong because its route to the brain is on a one-way street.

The sexual sensation, the vagabond, can call no door its own—unlike the other senses, each posted at its own sense organ. The sexual sensation belongs to the whole body equally and is yet bodily nowhere in particular, the way matter belongs indifferently to the finite world and to eternity, and the way God is everywhere but in no single place.

Blinking eyelids bejewel the look. That face needs no adornment whose lids close and unclose like the voluptuous wings of a wounded bird.

Sexual enjoyment is pleasure in the round. If the Serpent had divided the apple, sexual enjoyment would never have come into the world.

The sexual act is a game of leap-frog in which the leaper always lands on the frog whose back he tries to clear. If he ever succeeded in bounding over it he would fall into the next world. Death is the obstacle cleared, life's victorious leap.

Falling forward is, in a sense, wanting to fall; as falling backward—under the remote control of the cerebellum—is largely subconscious. Falling on your back means partial anesthesia.

Dull sounds penetrate the cranium at dead center from on high, sharp sounds penetrate at the sides. Stay near a waterfall for a good long time and the sound will bore a hole through your head. Shrill noises eventually plane away at the temples. Headaches are the result of the head's being a "sounding" board.

The soul enjoys the sensual world at a certain remove, feeding and eliminating osmotically. Only at the peak of venereal excitement does it come in close like horse and rider squeezing together at the height of the gallop.

The sick tree's roots "branch" out even as its branches "root" down. In the burning fever of a profound illness, our legs turn to arms and our arms turn to legs, reverting us somewhat to our animal state in which arms and legs are indifferently members of the same body.

A relaxed body and tranquil mind clarify the breath, separating and settling its odors like some undisturbed emulsion in a jar.

Conception would be impossible unless the mating of a couple allowed for some sort of psychic interference. If the souls of two bodies joined in the act of love were completely mingled, the infant soul would be "inhibited" at the moment of its expression into life. There would be no place for the baby to exist as soon as it issued from the limbs of its parents. Fortunately, this simply does not happen. The great generative spasm of conception is always present to keep the participating souls miles apart, leaving all the space required for the newborn to flow into existence.

We never feel that nature is excessive in anything because color and form are so completely connected: button and buttonhole adjusted by divine fingers. Only manufactured objects strike us as being excessive in one way or another, and this arises from the fact that either the buttonhole is too tight or the button "swims" in its moorings.

In the theater showing the performance of love we are both actor and spectator of ourselves, and all the seats are in the first row. If we had to peer at ourselves, so to speak, over the shoulders of anyone else, our soul would break our neck in the effort and simply pass into the other world. Isn't that what we usually mean by death?

In man the act of love is a one-room house; in woman it is a beehive.

There are no protective railings to the act of love. The twoness of oneness is the railings themselves.

The act of love is a toboggan in which those who are joined become each other's vehicle.

Forms are means, ideas are ends. But most books are maze dances of gorgeous words with no place to go, twisting and turning human thought as if human thought were not dizzied enough already. The only worthwhile books are those that simplify life.

The act of love is the sensation of *double concavity*, as if the earth we walked on began to slip away underfoot so that at each descending step the foot seemed to touch down twice. While we are making love our nerves intersect each other, doubling the exposure of all our sensory hollows and openings, like two crossed fingers of one hand touching a marble in the palm of the other hand.

If you're looking for love's whereabouts, ask Smell, the nearest relative. Just as women weaken under their own perfumes, so all physical loving begins in an olfactory swoon. Doesn't Death follow a parallel trajectory, with the final sweep of the scythe signalled by some gust of perfume from the Afterworld?

What changes the expression of a face more than anything else is the color of a hat or collar, of a ribbon or a scarf or a jacket, complementing the pigment of the eye, creating a total visual effect seen impressionistically at a distance. If we could some day discover a substance that would change the pigment of the iris as a dye colors our hair, it would make an astounding mask, camouflaging the soul as well as the face.

The babbling brook struck by a headlong gust of wind chokes the sounds deep down into its throat until the liquid lips emit a human cry.

It is impossible for the sense of smell to choose which "flower" to concentrate on in any mixed bouquet of odors that assails the nostrils: it grabs the whole bunch. If smell really tried to choose it would either strangulate or lose them all. The sexual act, like smelling, is a group sense in which peripheral pleasures cling inextricably to the main ones. If venery could ever twist its head around during its progress forward it would find itself transformed like Lot's wife into a salt statue equivalent. Gone would be its primary form and divine substance.

One sound adds to another. What you taste now subtracts from all previous tastes. Smells when they mix multiply each other. The quotient of skin pressing closer and closer to skin is your sense of touch. Sight is the algebraic sum of colors.

The voice of water is the human voice thrummed like a taut membrane.

Separated in the world of things, colors have group sex on the retina. Think of it this way: if there were no light, nothing could exist; hence, everything is "sex." What painting actually amounts to is the fashioning of the picture surface into a second retina so that the intercourse of the colors might be doubly visible to the eye's beholding.

Lovemaking begins with a face to face meeting of single souls and ends up back to back, the communion at the outset changing into the strange aloofness of after-sex.

The longest-handled rake is the look of the eye.

A laugh is a yawn that rolls along on a ratchet; a yawn is a smooth laugh. Mix the two and the effect is faintly that of a horse whinnying. Is the horse's neigh his laugh or his yawn?

Some types of human laughter can even express boredom. The horse's neigh is boredom trying to laugh. In the animal kingdom all the various ways of expressing emotion are connected. The sound is essentially the same sound whether initiated by laughter or weeping, sneezing or snorting, belching or coughing. The sound differs only in form according to how long the note is held.

Lovemaking shapes the brain into a kind of rump—so completely spherical that it can only *sit* there. The act of love encodes our nerves and tissues with a sensation of absolute roundness: the god-image.

Space is Many, not One. If space were One, the soul would have to crumple the body like an accordion in order to find room enough to move around in under the influence of the feelings. If our two yoked eyes remained effortlessly open in normal position instead of turning in on themselves at the culminating point of lovemaking, they would force space to do the splits and instantly shape all nature into a big V.

We never yield ourselves completely in the act of love. The carnal egoism that holds us back serves either one of the coital pair as a buffer against the other. Otherwise the soul of each would flow into the body of the other in instantaneous metempsychosis, and body and soul would become diluted into each other by osmosis.

Lovemaking is cyclical or nothing. Think of all the women who have to be satisfied with a ninety degree turn all their lives because their partners insist on making the whole circuit on their own.

Silence is as shapeless as space is unlimited. Like space, silence is consubstantial with everything.

In the kiss all the colors and all the sounds wheel past in succession one by one and over and over. The act of love is blue silence.

Absolute newness is total nakedness.

Writing slows down the *qualitative,* speech slows down the *quantitative* development of language. Abolish writing for a thousand years and the alphabet will have doubled its lettristic resources after it emerges from the eclipse and to that extent will have improved its encoding powers.

Indifference turns the pupil's brilliant glow into a night-light of a look.

A pistol shot begins as a bastinade and ends in a whip flick.

In eating, the lower lip turns into a perfect bib, the upper lip into a napkin. It's because babies are so unaccustomed to using their lips that they fail to catch the dribble properly and try to chew with their "bibs."

The diamond is the light's hen who laid the golden egg.

The mouth ages morally more rapidly than it does physically, and the opposite is true of the eyes. The materialism that wears away a man's ideals wears down the expression of the mouth in most of us quicker than it affects the eyes. If materialism continues to bulk larger in our futures, then sooner or later a day will come when the eyes and mouth in the same face will look as if they belonged to two different beings, a set of features with a double head.

Progress keeps offering us more comfort, comfort softens us further, and the habit of a soft life demands even more comfort. This is the vicious circle to send us down on all fours again until we turn into slugs, those creeping softnesses of least effort.

Up to a point eating is like walking. The body's general gait describes a kind of interior motion consubstantial with all our other movements.

The lower lip smiles more widely, the upper lip more expansively. The laugh is always a notch further up on the face than the smile.

Fog rounds out sounds. Fogbound voices seem full of blithe spirits.

Mouth askew: clubfooted laugh.

Undress in an open field. Nature, duplicating your own "state of nature," will make you feel twice as naked. Think now of how the act of love suffuses us with the sensation of having "less than" nothing on when it strips our senses as it bares our souls.

Intelligence lengthens the compass arms of the brain but only intuition can force those arms open. What good are the longest arms in the world if they still adhere to the trunk? A few flashes of insight do more for the world than several centuries of culture.

We tend to lean forward over the brook in order not to miss a syllable of its babbling; and to tilt our head back in order to take in every "breath" of the orchestra's effluvium: in man-made music each emerging sound puts the finishing touch to each receding one, whereas nature's music is a phosphorescent trail in which each sound we are hearing has already slipped beyond earshot, being part of our ears' "second sight" at the very moment our hearing first seizes it.

Hardly a change in the sun that the moon doesn't reflect or any trail across the expanse of the human countenance that the mouth doesn't reveal in some small way.

Space is the widest open of all mouths.

The act of love starts on its heathenish way to end up blessed by a transfixing spasm from the world beyond.

Silk makes colors slip and glide. A lithe body clad in silk makes a lovely tableau vivant of skating forms executing figures.

A stiff gait turns the hips into a hobble skirt. Nude female performers wear their own skins so tightly that they can't walk without mincing steps. Nudity must learn to yield itself to the air before it can become its own master. Let it look to smoke for instruction, which submits its form, body and soul, to the wind-god's will.

If dictators only knew how to subdue themselves, they wouldn't need to conquer the world. Self-rule is the real object of authoritarian hysteria.

The face achieves perfect unity only at arms' length, the minimum distance for white of eye, iris, and pupil to coalesce. Otherwise the face remains divided and the expression is seen only in sections. The observer's eye needs a good deal of impressionistic talent to make anything of another's facial expression.

God is all nakedness, the essence of nakedness. God clothes everything but what can he wear? When we talk about self-regeneration we mean divesting ourselves of everything, totally, until we can begin to resemble our Maker.

The human voice is the sun of sound at its zenith.

The perfect painting says exactly what it means no matter how symbolic its imagery. The ideal book has the clarity of a picture book.

The horse's leap was created in the wave's image. The sea in motion is the steeplechase of the absolute. If all the horses in an obstacle course hurdled the barrier in one surge, they would make an ocean out of ripplings.

Marriage is the spigot on the heart's waterpipe. Single life means that the feelings gush endlessly without ever being opposed or renewed, like a free flow of water desperately seeking to embrace the air that will not give in.

The Cyclops amounts to a mythical report of a psychic fact: the overpowering look of certain unearthly and indomitable men whose eyes merge like crossed swords at the meeting point of forehead and nose bridge. When the hypnotized subject goes under, he has already been knocked out unawares by the sledgehammer of this single eye. In the world of the absolute, God's outward glance is one-eyed: witness that supreme image of divinity, the single stare of the sun.

The aging process affects the ears later than any of the other features: only in advanced old age do ears begin to look older than twenty. If our ears declined at the same rate as the rest of us, a man would turn thirty looking like his simian ancestors, since it's the ears that most make us resemble animals. Nothing crumples the face up like a pair of horny old ears. Or, to put it another way, all animal faces—bar none—look like unmade beds compared to the smooth fit of human features on their facial frame.

In the act of love woman breathes from her pelvis, man from his shoulder hollows. This accounts for love's taut bowstring effect, bow and string in mutual dependence ready to loose the shivering arrows of delight.

The eye's pupil is at eternal noon.

The model of marching in step is the rhythmical bounce of the female breasts.

The sense of beauty is affected by history and varies according to change and fashion. Charm alone, from yesterday until the end of time, remains golden and invariable.

The wind keeps ever raising the leaf's hand to his lips until the hurricane takes over with his fingertip-to-armpit kisses, a lover so amorous of his mistress's flesh that he wants to banquet on the entire arm.

Autumn leaves falling and twirling in the wind combine the knee stomp of witch doctors with the shimmying of houris. They unite the ballet steps of operatic sylphs with the head gestures of Hindu priests. Nothing makes our brain dance in our senses so much as the sight of leaves falling. If you fix your attention for a long time on leaves as they fall, on their total embodiment of dance movements, the superhypnotic spell is so penetrating that you soon forget life itself. You experience an inexplicable feeling of reincarnation, as if you had become all leaves, like Narcissus forgetting himself to the point of thinking he was the water his eyes saw.

Smells get so familiar that they force us to edge away. Smell is utter intimacy, nothing but hands all over us, the ultimate privacy of the touch in touching. Think of the violation in the smell of all the people around us every minute of our lives. Smell takes over possessiveness itself, turning space into hands.

Clothed as they are in gestures, our fingers hide their feelings. Our palms are as naked as light itself, communicating with the core of the brain. Hence the remarkable truthfulness of the lines of the hand and the miraculous imposition of Christ's hands—the palms leading to God—by which the Man-God works all his miracles. Do we not assign extraordinary importance to the gesture of blessing, to the total contact of the handshake, to the simple avowal of the hand raised in oath, to the useless washing of Pilate's hands (the palm being incapable of lying), and to the exposure of the Divine Palm on the cross, a palm whose supreme death throes shine like a lighthouse in the night of God's agony? Denude your gestures, your voice, and your step, and you will feel yourself dressed in light.

The palm of the hand is your sex stripped bare—but even more, your whole body and soul in little, all the concentrated splendor of the living self, the mind's invariability as well as its humors. No "fig-leaf" could cling to the hand without those high voltage wires, the palm's network of lines, consuming it in the instant, the way a blast furnace would incinerate a single sheet of paper.

When the feelings are calm, the eyes breathe and the mouth flutters and when they are upset, the lips breathe and the look flutters. If lungs and heart did not extend their double control over life's essential functions into the face itself, the human countenance would be a lump of flesh with the features expressing chaotic signals.

The leaf is all profile; the flower can never be anything but full face no matter what angle you view it from. If both were profiles the flower would seem to be riding the leaf like a horseman; and if both were full face the whole plant would flatten out into a kind of tapestry. So long as the leaf's flatness is wedded to the flower's fullness, we tend to see flowers superimposed on leaves even when the foliage is in the foreground. Because of this a plant's leaves never "drown out" its flowers. The full face always seems nearer than the profile even at the same distance away.

Make a carpet of millions of inconceivably thin needles massed together point upward and you'll find it possible to relax on its prickly resilience without the least apprehension. Its infinitely multiplied tinglings actually offer the highest tactile delights. The act of love is lying on such a carpet woven of tightly packed grains of pain and pleasure.

In our world of effects here below, quality and quantity are superimposed ideas, extraneous to the nature of things. In the world of causes beyond our own, quality "swells up" into quantity, the idea of the latter being an emanation of the former.

Corpuscles of the human body.
Ovule.
Foetus tucked up into itself in the uterus.
Curled up ball of a sleeping infant.
The spherical voluptuousness of the act of love.
The shrivelled up hunch of extreme old age.
The spherical idea, the God-image, is found at the poles of life.

The eyelids define the aristocracy of the face. Just the slightest twitch of its eye would make Apollo's stony visage lopsided, the way a vase with one handle gone looks lopsided in sunlight.

The touch of the ring finger is curved and hollow. The thumb's touch is rounder than that of any other finger. When the two come together, the thumb seems to fit inside the ring finger. Consider the same contrast on the piano where the thumb "sorts out" sounds that are "packed away" by the fourth finger, respectively a kind of sonic paying out and paying in of "funds." The fourth finger is a little harmonic dam which keeps sounds from overflowing and spilling off.

A man limping tends to walk like a three-footed animal—describing the kind of movement any creature would have to make if it had three legs to walk with. All disharmony of the body gives the effect of threeness, breaking down its symmetry by the adjunction of a third member.

Green, garnet, purple, and mauve are all suspended in space by blue straps. No matter how mixed colors get, if there's any blue in them it floats on top. Without blue's powers of survival as the brace between heaven and earth all the colors would seem to be superimposed on the blue of the sky rather than being incorporated in it, and all nature would be a picturebook rather than life's volume of living pictures.

Varnish is light tap-dancing. The diamond is light in high heels. A diamond riviere raises the neck, lending the head an aristocratic turn.

When the voice hesitates, the look falters in the eye. Whatever transpires in the world of the mouth is reflected in the eyes and vice-versa.

Trace lines between all the solar and planetary systems and the design will end as a gigantic skeleton—the essence of iconic God—the flesh of space filled out by dazzling suns, overflowing the interstices of everything all together, offering itself like a Towering Man in the retina of God.

The wind's inner voice is a millstone grinding itself. The sound of the wind smooths all kinds of voices.

The green of leaves at early dawn creates in us a sensation of mauve. The eye sees green but the soul sees mauve. The interior realities of colors are absolutely unrelated to their exterior realities. The spiritual body is color-blind to the physical body. If we actually saw blue in our soul at the same time as we saw blue in nature, the fusion would be so complete between mind and body that we would suffocate like the strangling man who must live on the pocket of air in his lungs.

A woman's breast is an apple within a pear, tipped by a grape. The ultimate blending: all the fruits in one.

Objects and things are needles to the wind's phonograph record, the human ear being the rest of the apparatus.

Absolute hardness would be the touch of absolute cold, and absolute softness would be the sensation experienced by cold as it touched, like the touching of a corpse capable of feeling. Beyond a certain degree of consistency, hardness and softness are expressible only as temperature.

Prevision is a series of telescopes facing into each other with a real eye looking through every single one of them. To penetrate the past in the same way substitute microscopes for telescopes.

The act of love is entertainment for one's entire being, soul, body, and infra-body—all three—feasting at the same table.

What makes it the most perfect of all enjoyments is that even if the courses are different for each of the three guests they all still eat from the same plate. Moreover, the reason nature is a communion is that all enjoyments are connected to the same joy, all the diners are there together sharing the same "spread."

Rolling of the hips—like cheeks stifling and gasping—is the loudest laughter. Children swaying as they stand up tall: their hips smile.

Kissing is each mouth suckling the other. The act of love is three-way suckling: two "mouths" at the same feeding-cup.

The tongue touches pliant foods like the fourth finger of the hand. Anything sour it approaches like the little finger. The tongue turns into an index finger, directing food to the teeth whenever they are reluctant to begin chewing, and it thrusts food out of the mouth like a thumb. It becomes a middle finger in order to curl round thick, soft masses of food.

Salt fills up the cracks in food. When a dish lacks salt our sense of taste has to feel its way along carefully in order not to stumble.

Making love consists of both the idea and the feeling of death and of birth, not as juxtaposed cords parallel to each other but twisted together just enough so that we can't really tell whether the ecstasies of love are truly killing us or really bringing us to birth.

The act of love is two living bodies squeezing and hugging a corpse. The corpse, here, is the body of time itself, momentarily eliminated to become consubstantial with the sense of touch.

The act of love projects us for a time into the Great Beyond like a slide valve in operation at the edge of a cliff. Death is an overhang that slides forward and then lets drop: the hanged man's last orgasm.

The act of love turns the spinal column into a finger as if to feel and caress the brain from within.

When we're wide awake, space before our eyes seems larger than space behind us. With our eyes shut the reverse seems truer. Lateral space is the smallest of all types of space. Why? Because the human face is the Pole of Light, the human back the Pole of Darkness, and we cannot effectively see in front and in back of our body day or night.

The act of love transfigures the eye and develops a halo around the mouth.

We seek out blue, yellow comes to us. The ray of light comes to us; we must seek out the azure sky. A yellow dress gives itself to us; blue asks to be taken. Yellow is for women in love; blue for available widows.

The sexual act deflates the imagination—people always seem stupider afterward.

We refuse to recognize in the Devil all those aspects of God that we don't understand. As a result the Devil is much more mysterious than God Himself.

The sun is the best of all couturiers but the moon is the better shoe stylist—its light is heavier and lies lower to the ground than sunlight, hugging and clinging to the toes and heels of the earth's flora, whereas the sunlight lets their nakedness shine through.

To accentuate the gaiety of flowers, make a bouquet of them, although this reduces their individual distinctions. The more heterogeneous the crowd, the more vulgar will it appear.

The eye is the most perfect of slates. Anything chalked on it eventually fades, what was clearly visible just a moment ago has simply disappeared a moment after, and yet some of its inscriptions are unmistakably still and always there.

Space is the haunches of the Universe, the essential principle of matter being the sex of God—all life is the product of his semination—while the rest of his Body remains forever concealed from us. We will never know where exactly God can be marked present or where his mind dwells: the Alpha and Omega forever lost in God Himself. Born in his face, we die in his back. If God received us at death in the fullness of his face, our impure substance would be utterly consumed by the fire of his eyes. This explains why the light of his Holy Spirit is more blinding on the face of the squalling infant than on the countenance of man at his last gasp.

If the soul woke up inside a cadaver that refused to budge, the torment of its anguish would make the anguish of a natural death seem like playing. Yet think of all the madmen in the world flailing around in their dissociated bodies whose seizures almost split their beings apart and who at those moments feel as if their souls were screaming to be let out of a sealed coffin—men who live through ten thousand deaths every second, each more terrifying than real death, before the death of the body releases them from this Hell. To cut short its suffering we dispatch the horse that breaks its leg. Are we ever going to dispatch certain kinds of madmen whose brains are so far beyond repair that whatever hope the future might hold for rekindling the divine light of their intelligence, animals are actually rational creatures by comparison? Heaven and Earth are riven apart in such mad creatures, as if an angel's mirror reflected a reptile or slug staring back at him, or for that matter, a slug were forced to see himself an angel. In either case there is no possibility of escaping his double self that stretches him out between Heaven and Earth, crucifies him along the whole length of his nature and on all the planes of his being.

The upper lip is the general in command of the mouth. The lower lip always follows his superior into the battle zone of emotion. When the reverse takes place on the human countenance it is almost always the sign of sexual inversion or a level of subnormal sexuality close to atony.

No humor as dry as hip-humor with its softly muffled laughter from inside the body. The hips jiggle up and down with a coldly mocking sense of pleasure.

If, after long and exacting application, we ever reached the point of separating our brains into sections—as we might imagine doing with the food we eat—tasting the salt while we untaste the pepper, isolating the ginger at the expense of the garlic, taking complete advantage of the allspice while ignoring the parsley —the effect of this discipline would have so great a repercussion on our total sensory awareness—since all our senses are interconnected—that with respect to our vision alone we would come to view the world as if through the slits of a peephole. Now although this "system" would hardly change our actual appearance, it would influence our eyesight so much that we would see asquint at the eye's center without any torsion of the eye itself. The pupil, in other words, would be so browbeaten by the brain's constant demands that it would seem to take refuge in the iris's territory as in some of Picasso's terrifying faces.

Because they have no lips to modulate sounds with, birds can only speak in "throat impulses." Because they have never known the use of their lips, babies can only make birdlike sounds.

Light-dazzle jacks up space, adding a second storey to our view of things. Indeed, space keeps piling up levels as the breadth of our look increases. Imagine what would happen otherwise: our eyes would tend to see any sudden brilliance of light from behind rather than in front, in a soft of fourth-dimensional perspective that would turn us all into seers.

No animal knows its creaturely job better than the butterfly, who cannot even imagine making a winged mistake. All her wing beats are measured and certain; even her apparently indecisive ventures are born of assurance. When butterflies look as if they were hesitating they are really playing hide-and-seek with the wind to gain time.

Fear decomposes the breath like Russian dressing unmaking itself and returning to its elements.

Light-dazzle is the sun's kick-back: keep looking at it and the moonlight in it floods into view.

You cannot have sympathetic magic unless both magician and victim are at the mercy of the powerful forces binding them together, the latter unaware of the profound effects transforming him, the former equally unaware of what precisely he has conjured up in Hell's or Heaven's name. If it were otherwise, the "spell" would break, the invisible bonds slacken. Witchcraft is a current leaping from one pole to another in an energy transmission whose primary source is no less obscure to the witch than it is the bewitched. They are communicating vessels both, the witch receiving spiritual messages and then transmitting them to the bewitched, who discharges them in turn—but neither ever knows when the message is complete or when he has finished "saying" it. The flow goes on independent of the agent's control, nor has the magician any way of telling when the victim's vessel is full. Only when the latter suddenly cracks and breaks from the unchecked volume of the psychic flow, only then when it is too late to shut the valves does the magician wake up to realize what has passed through them both.

    The look in the eye of a forceful man overpowers us so that we lose consciousness of his face, our faculties clouded by his glance. We may even recoil so far as to forget he has a body, all life else shrinking momentarily from our eyes. Now imagine this remarkable power of his look to the point of supernatural possibility and what you have at last is that physiological wizardry so long sought after: the invisible man.

    In eyes with tawny or dark irises the pupil looks as if it were screwed into place, just as eyes with pale irises look as if their pupils were nailed in. This explains the fixed stare of eyes with light irises, which hold you in a steadier gaze than irises of darker color. Heighten the pallor of such irises and they develop the "nailed-in" look of pearl buttons with black centers.

    The paw of an animal is a tool box, but he doesn't know very much about using its contents. A man's hand is an empty box in which tools keep materializing. This is why an animal's walk sometimes seems so awkward, why human gestures often look so magical.

    Light shining on water droplets spaced out along a bamboo stalk turns the whole structure into a flute.

From a distance sounds heard in single file become flute-toned.

The one-holed flute sounds like the highest reach of a violin.

An orchestra tends to "whistle" sounds that are strung out one after another: music that makes you grit your teeth.

Brilliance is an indigestion of light and the vomitorium of the sun. Brilliance without pause nauseates us. Nothing could be worse than seasickness at high noon.

Touching is always sexual no matter how fond or innocent the gesture. There's no such thing as an insignificant kiss. If there were, the lips would recoil as soon as they tallied, the skin would refuse to exert itself, and the muscles in turn would go on strike. Sexuality is inherent in all our gestures, inextricably part of all aspects of life.

The wave is the most female of all dancers, the wind the most male. In their dance of space the wave is all hip and haunch, the wind all-embracing.

Supersensitive beings feel themselves touched before they actually are, "thrill" to the approach of the body that promises heavenly delights. If our physical and psychic antennae were only powerful enough all that our hands would need to do would be to draw near to the sensitive flesh that waits for their touch and it would already be relaxed in satisfaction long before the touch was completed.

The woman lucky enough to have eyelashes as long and as silky as a thicket of ferns can be proud of not needing earrings or other facial ornaments. Lashes such as hers are like pendants capable of illuminating all the features and accentuating the scenic beauty of the expression as well.

The essence of the human face lies in the intimate connection between mouth and eyes when the soul trembles peculiarly or is deeply moved. The essence of the animal face is the very absence of relation between mouth and eye, which are totally separate and divorced. An animal's eye at times is more human than a man's, but its mouth is still animal in form, construction, and final nature. The mouth of the most perfect human brute is a thousand godly miles away from the most "angelic" animal mouth. Because of the almost complete absence of spiritual intelligence in its mouth, we must persist in believing that the animal's soul lies "on another plane," although we would favorably compare certain animal glances with the best of human glances.

In double flowers the inner petals would seem to be as bunchy and irregular as the outer ones are elegantly simple. See to it, my dear, that your wrap is as reticent as your gown is showy.

The eye would never be able to take its motion pictures without the fourth dimension of the brain. The less of an artist you are, the more your eye registers everything as if it were flat. A man's inability to gauge distance is almost always a sign that he looks at the world bluntly, straight from the shoulder, without any of his own resources to draw upon. This defect of vision is something he projects outward by tending to rake the landscape inward, to appropriate it a little rudely. This, of course, is what egoists always do with the breathless grasping of their spiritual myopia.

The eye is the smallest of all pieces of furniture. Rest and relaxation make you sprawl out in your eye as if it were a couch. To awaken someone's interest don't we often have to separate him from his eye as if we were pulling him by the arm out of an overstuffed chair?

Widely spaced pores make the skin look more naked. Unlimited nakedness, boundless nakedness, would give us the sensation of the absolute as flesh. Nakedness must be impure, must be finite in order to exist at all. This finiteness, which limits, fixes, and defines nakedness is the sexuality of things. Without pores—those smallest of all sexual vessels—the skin would be a total and infinite vestment.

The breasts are varnished, the haunches are lacquered, the arms are waxed, the belly is polished. But the texture of the thighs is of raw silk, tightly stretched over the pores to keep those tiny carnal jewels from unnecessary contact, more or less as its shell protects the snail from needless friction.

Man's eye sees an object by *filling* it with sight, whereas his mouth sees by *sucking in* the seen world. Woman's mouth, on the other hand, is convex in apprehension; her eye is concave. Women are trapped by looks, men by mouths, in a kind of facial ball and socketing like bifid copulation.

The act of love is the occiput capable of touch.

We do not "see" space because it already belongs to our eyes. Space is a *state* common to all forms of life, not a *place* which permeates everything. If space were localized it would look back at us with eyes of its own. That return glance of something additional to itself would be so unnerving and absolute that sight *would disappear* into the sense of touch and we be struck blind by its devouring ocularity. The target of all eyes blankly loses consciousness of his surroundings.

The sound of water is the matrix of all imaginable sounds—all except the whistle—that exclusively man-made sound—which forms a right angle as it leaves its launching platform. Man is the only creature who can make a flute-hole of his mouth.

A swarm of insects turns on its own axis hurtling forward at tremendous speeds, yet why is it the insects never touch—let alone collide? Surely not because insects have the most highly developed sense of direction of all living beings: what about all those heedless little creatures that smash into the most unmistakable obstacles like a blind man the first time he ventures out? The swarm's uncanny awareness of what the air lanes will permit is more than simply a sense of direction; if anything it is a collective sense of direction belonging to a sixth sense independent of hive and horde—coming from a master control center that maneuvers the swarm from some unseen point, guiding each insect as if it were a robot. What makes this explanation likely is the way in which an insect swarm veers now right, now left, in its course like two hands kneading dough.

Shadow follows behind light like a carriage behind a horse in necessary agreement with its momentum. In all of nature "quicksilver" shadows exist only in the human glance, where the eyes' firelight is both shadow and substance, as if the carriage were the burden on the beast's back.

Space is the result of innumerable concavities badly adjusted to each other. Space is the holes in hollowness.

Nostrils too sharply curved do something to the main rib of the nose as if a cheap trinket were hanging on the mouth. Imagine this peculiarity in a more deforming state and from a distance it would look like a harelip. Anything that deforms the nose from side to side cuts into the mouth, just as the acute accent over the letter makes it bleed.

Our skin tends to feel scorched under the play of certain kinds of breath as if they were the agents of some spiritual force. How strange that the Devil's mouth should be thought of as a furnace when his breath is icy! It's the Angel, whose breath is flaming, whose mouth burns with love.

From the indented corners of the mouth to the bosoming fullness at the center of the mouth, the lips pass through all degrees of lustrousness gradually rising in brilliance, as the sea ranges from sparkling waves along the coast to a great watery sun at the harbor's mouth.

Man's face would still be human if his mouth were in a different place but not if his eyes were reassigned; for the mouth is a satellite of the eye's sun and no star can be eccentric to its planet's center.

Animals are never professionally pedantic or boring, because they are born into their vocations. You can tell a true professional by his willingness to talk about anything under the sun.

Death is the most all-engaging work imaginable—the dying man is literally head over heels involved in his "travail" in the most absolute sense of the term, so that were the soul to re-awaken immediately it would hardly be surprising to find it all tired out. There is a hidden wisdom in the Gospel's allowing for three days of rest between death and resurrection.

No matter how much the rest of the body ages, the hips never lose their youthfulness. How could the hips wear themselves out, since they serve as the whole body's director's chair of flesh? If it ever collapsed we would simply give way like a subsiding meringue.

Green water has blue fingers and a green palm. Let your eyes skim over the green of water and the sensation will be one of blue. Rest your eye upon that same expanse and your glance will "swim" in green.

The meridians of mind, heart, and senses never meet concentrically. If they did, man would "fuse" into himself and melt under the converging effects of the noonday fires of these coexisting suns. Man would lose his perspective point for estimating all living experience, unable to perceive any feelings at all—as a wheel placed in its *absolute* axis would lose all relationship to its own circumference.

Rub two pieces of wood together long enough and a spark flies out. Under the influence of a steady gaze the eye becomes phosphorescent.

The ideas of weight and volume vary with the areas of the body, according to their unevenness or consistency. And the ideas of hollowness or fullness are directly related to those of weight and volume. The reason we attach a yoke to the neck of oxen is to translate something of the idea of weight into that of volume. We drag along human cattle by the shoulder for the same reason. The jar borne on the head weighs less than it would anywhere else on the body since our head gives us the most striking sensation of volume that we can have of our bodies.

By means of radioactive particles mixed with the crystals of a glass to make it invisible, and by the future atomic possibilities of making water itself radioactive, a full decanter will look like a formless suspension of water. The decanter will be conjured away by the effect of light rays. Sitting down to dinner, we shall grow accustomed to seeing on the tablecloth, instead of a flower-designed vase, minute aerial pools sewn with roses, violets, or lilies, like the hanging gardens of Aladdin. A thousand forms of life will float by themselves. The invisible era is now underway, the era of atomic invisibility. The very idea of weight will be done away with. By means of atomic glasses we shall be able to see through matter as if it were made of crystal. More than this, atomic telescopes will reveal the other ends of the universe, the extreme confines of the visible world. The atomic era will perhaps not put us physically in touch with Mars, but with the sight of it from close by, despite the immensity of the ether separating us, so that we may expect to see Mars, as it were, window to window, just as we now see people across an alley.

Smells make animals dance in head movements that often enough end in their toes. The dances of primitive peoples are all designed to imitate this animal model of Nature's gestures, as in the head dance performed by Hindu priests around the fragrance of the incense burner. The gods of all times and places have been better pleased by the smell of burnt offerings than by any other kind of adoration. With their truly "sacred" notion of smells animals are actually more "religious" than we are.

The human backside is always restraining the softer fleshes from escaping its elastic packing case. We never really wear our own hips, we are forever dragging them along with us. A girdle or corset converts these pillories of flesh into their own chaise-longue.

In the silence of the night walls cry out. In the silence of the act of love our whole frame cracks with the clamoring of our bones, like a man in agony venting the cry of his crumbling frame, like the newborn baby who feels its bones crack as its body soars into life, like a schooner cracking with skeletal tautness as its sails take the first sea-borne gusts.

Looked at point-blank the mouth is more striking a "creature" than the eye—as the liplike eyelids seen up close look more like soft little beings than the eyes themselves.

The moon is anti-light in the absolute. Look fixedly at the sun and you will eventually "see" white night.

The gestures of the feet are perhaps the most "artificial" part of our step. Our feet have no "natural" gestures except in water. The watery element is the greatest of all simplifiers of gesture. All the gestures of the fish are infantile.

Bitterness so shatters the unity of our sense of taste that the tongue has to send out tonguelets to recover it.

The bourgeois is a man with no history, is as unhistorical as God himself; the one is pure emptiness, the other pure repletion. The bourgeois is a living foetus that never comes of age spiritually. In the afterworld he will probably be the kind of child-man that some rustics are on earth.

All flowers wear low-necked gowns. No space is more naked than the air between two petals—like the petal-like opening between two breasts, which is the ultimate in dress disclosures.

Grass turning yellow on the slopes makes the mountain seem steeper than before—for colors have their own slopes, yellow being the steepest. Yellow lifts up middle-aged hips but at the expense of flattening out sagging breasts. Two-piece dresses are called for after forty, an age when a woman's body needs the firmness of colors, an age when the body can no longer serve color proudly as a flagbearer.

The mouth's moods vary more rapidly than the eyes'. Women's eyes are monthly, their mouths daily.

The breath is like an insect in that its flight goes every which way, a sort of butterfly-fragrance. Can you ever tell whose breath it is in a crowd as it glances by? It might be coming from anywhere. The breath of the woman you love wafts itself in the air you inhabit like a volatile caress.

The human eye, the moon, the sun. Triple-faced mirror of the Absolute.

Space is time at its most elusive; like woman, always there when you're not particularly concerned with it, but as soon as you try to avoid it, space hounds you.

The immutable look of the sun: God hasn't blinked his eyes even once in all eternity.

All flowers have two eyes like us, but one is on the obverse, the other on the reverse side. On the obverse the flower's eye is wide open, on the reverse its lids are lowered—but as with the eye of the seraph its gaze burns on behind the apparent curtain. The reason flowers have no real back and front is that their back-to-back eyes make a circular face.

The little finger has a microscopic sense of touch, the index finger has a telescopic sense of touch. If you want to examine the bulkiness of a grain of sand, you feel it over and over with the little finger; but to locate a crack or hollow in a wall what else would you want to use except the index?

Nothing makes the whole face more liquid than the smile which turns it into the cradle of the sea itself. An angelic smile is the eye bobbing softly on the waves of the expression.

Channel a stream, deflect it sharply downhill, and you have a torrent. There are writers who owe their success to the combination of a limited vocabulary and a harsh style, the effect of which is to speed up the ideas in the narrow channel of the words. This is where all their power and persuasion comes from.

The freedom to be yourself is the highest form of justice toward others, whereas the impersonal justice of judges is the greatest, most dangerous threat to individual liberty: the judge becomes a bullet without conscience in the rifle of the Law. The man who is not himself is incapable of doing justice to himself or to others because he sucks the moral freedom he lacks from the social body that gave him birth. He represents a kind of muscular contraction that siphons off freedom from other parts of the body in order to do its little jig.

Space is the air in the balloon of matter, the pneuma of all things. A mere balloon flight from here into the realm of spirit—from the world of effects into the realm of causes—would make a flat bladder of the entire living world, an empty, structureless, uninformed body; and the living world would go on lifeless through eternity like an unalive foetus in the infinite uterus of time.

Fog is the wind's overcoat: the only way the wind can keep from being wet through by the water is to make it into an outer covering. Fools are your only protection against fools: the sluggish kind are your buffer against the aggressive ones. The fog keeps the air from being rained on.

Flowing water is an inverted troop camp, all the orders being given from the bottom up. It's the "tail" that's in charge of the brook. The river's brains are in its source, the fire's are in the already burning brand that tells the flame tips which way to fork. In nature the general earns his stars according to his place in the scale of things, not his cleverness at commanding.

No madman is completely mad in both eyes at the same time, no sensible man completely reasonable in both eyes at once. One eye is always "fooling around" while the other means what it looks. The eyes are a balance jittering with counterweights.

Far from being the tersest syllable in the language, "I" is actually the most uncertain. In the most complete sense no one can be entirely himself: every "I" utterance is colored by the words around it. The first "I" you enunciate is never the same "I" that ends the sentence: like the kind of theorem that depends on a succession of arguments, no matter how much your later "I" develops it, your introductory "I" never reflects more than parts of yourself. Beware of people who love to talk about themselves, for they are truly the self-ignorant, constantly trying to see if their selves are still there. They have molten egos, capable of anything.

Colors relay sight. If nature were all one color, the eyes would be worn out long before sunset, and in order to recuperate from the effort, man would have to sleep twice as long as he does now. The more colorful the landscape, the more it rests your eyes. Modern eye-fatigue is the result of the unvaried greyness of our cities with their one-crop culture.

Color is the fat of fabrics; texture is the cartilage. On the invisible particles of brilliant white satin the light turns to bone. Imperceptible particles of certain white silks and satins bring out the framework of the forms they clothe, emphasize the structure of a well-made body. Hence the sacrament is inconceivable except as white, nor could Jesus Christ have worn any other color.

Natures too much alike repel each other. A house full of saints would amount to an insane asylum.

The stars are the pupils in the eyes of space. Without them the night sky would be as two-dimensional as the look of a blind man.

Moss is the absorbent cotton of plants which nature applies to its purulent parts.

Animals greet and address each other, express their thoughts and apostrophize—all with their tails. They carry on point-blank discourse by means of tail movements. They hold their tongues in reserve for long-distance communication. Women can be both eloquent and outrageously direct in polite gatherings with the verbal undulations of their hips, those springboards of their vanished tails.

Ah (a) is the oldest word in the language. *Oh* (o) is relatively recent. The origin of *o* from the slack lips of prehistoric man was the first indication of his ability to discipline his lips for speech. The superiority of Latin over the ancient barbaric tongues can be seen in its multiple use of the *u* sound, which requires a stronger effort to pronounce. Other vowels will come into existence in the far future when man learns to rely less on his throat and much more on his lips, "civilizing" his mouth in order to be better understood in the babble of cities.

In the dictatorship of the home the child is the only *pro tem* minister of state during the struggle for domination between husband and wife.

Sexual intercourse is the body's fine weather, the acme of good health, all the vital forces concentrated on the point of a needle. At the supreme height of sexual pleasure feeling sick would be meaningless, it no longer makes sense.

The crown of petals is the flower's panties. Rip them off and you have public indecency. They were the pre-adamic fig leaf of nature before the first Eve wore that leaf as her own crown of petals.

Old maids are sexual postal clerks who pillage the mails. Old maids are sexuo-spiritual dry-runners, like the miser who holds a piece of bread up against the cheese container hoping to extract some of the taste without using up the cheese.

Fear disengages your feelings from your thoughts. In a state of jealousy you tend to love in arrears. Othello never for a moment knew the Desdemona who was right there in front of him. It is because it confines love to the past that jealousy is proverbially so blind.

Fruit plucked too soon matures in patches, sweet parts right next to others still bitter. Girls who marry too young develop in enthusiasm and disillusion at the same rate: they are equally young and old at thirty, they become flighty in maturity, and they turn crabbed as well as childish in old age.

Space is the fourth dimension of matter, the spirituality of atomic particles. What we call time would seem to be nothing else than our spiritual life decelerating in the body until a thread forms between the two worlds.

Take off your jacket or dress and more of the soul will stick to it than remains in a just expired corpse. Cemeteries are fetishes laid out in rows, but a coat-and-hat rack is a living cemetery.

Religion is grabbing at an Idea on the banks of life to keep yourself from drowning. True believers plunge into the open sea to find God. True believers are born in the wide waters of spirituality as they leave the fading banks behind. True believers set sail for Infinity on the raft of life. No religion is the true faith unless it keeps following a restless star: God never stands still. If our religious ideas are unchangeable, our souls stagnate. To believe for all eternity in the same religion is to believe that the spiritual body has determined limits; but religion is not consubstantial with the soul but only the garment it wears.

Yellow is light's putty. Yellow noonday sun means seamless light, no grey cracks in the blue expanse, unending glossy azure, not a crease in the sky's nap, the scenery snugly in place on the skyline as on a sideboard.

The little finger initiates all the oblique gestures of the sense of touch and adds her initials to practically every movement of the hand. The female character, compounded as it is of afterthoughts and postscripts, shows its will to power clearly in the form of the little finger. Why do women let its nail grow so long if not to camouflage their will to power by trying to mislead the most alert eye concerning the little finger's shape and intentions? The purpose of the camouflage is to distract us from recognizing the little finger's symbolic nature.

The orchid is the one flower that absolutely refuses to mix. The worst snob of all the flora, the orchid stands out rudely wherever you put it. Stick an orchid into a bunch of other flowers and it upsets their balance instantaneously. Snobs go with snobs only. A bouquet of orchids has no place for any other flower.

Beige is orange beaten stiff. Dredge in blue, knead the paste, and you have grey.

The man who dies in spite of his desire to live is killed by a hand that suddenly appears from nowhere to pull the trigger on death's pistol; whereas the suicide presses the trigger all by himself. In this respect the suicide is like a pistol aimed at the afterlife, which is precisely why suicide is the greatest of all crimes against God. It is an attempt to wrest the initiative of life from the Creator, to violate the exclusiveness of the other world, by forcing an entry like an uninvited guest crashing a party who embarrasses the other guests as well as the host into a stony silence. Suicide is the greatest of crimes against the spirit because it is an attack on God. Where else, then, can the suicide go except back to the world below, since he has apparently been rejected by the world above? This would explain the Asiatic idea of metempsychosis, except that the East has carried it too far: the suicide has to be reborn on earth so that he may expiate his sin. The most appalling aspect of original sin is the hereditary taint attaching to suicide as expressed allegorically in the story of Cain's fratricide: an assault against the ego, which is brother to the immortal soul. Suicide is the supreme degree of spiritual incest.

Flowing oil is a mouth that dribbles its own bib like an endless tongue. Flowing oil never closes its lips as water does in order to take a breath.

The number four in the square is absolute separation, one divided pair—the opposite sides of the square—cutting off another. Couples in a square whose partners are face to face make conversation impossible. When you receive guests, put them in a quincunx at table in order to cut the conversation into facets, as one does with a diamond for greater brilliance.

The chicken "understands" the dog, the dog knows what the dove means, the insect can fathom the lowing of the cow, and the cow is always aware of the eagle's far approach. All audible animal messages are understood equally by all animals even though each one is monolingual at most. Could there be any more remarkable lesson in and example of understanding others without loss of personality? It should also be noted that people who have no personal language are the most impenetrable to the thoughts of others. Most intolerant people hail from the land of self-ignorance.

The joints of the body are the park benches of our sense of touch, where we can sit down sensually for a moment. Caresses at the joints fan out into a bodily tickling—sense perception playing the clown—which represents the small change of our caresses fallen into the vastness of our entire sensory deposit vault. They heighten the thirst of the nerves in the way a few drops of water in a gigantic glass would craze the parched mouth to bite into the glass and devour it.

In a strong wind the eyelids beat their wings like a bird launching into flight. A caged bird flutters its wings like smarting eyelids trying to free themselves from the cave of the eye. Fluttering eyelids fill the sky of the forehead with bird forms. When the world was created God's eyelids provided the breeding ground for all winged creatures and the allegorical motive for the wings of what we call angels: those beings of light who are closer than all other living creatures to the retina of the Lord so as to capture its rays at the source.

The act of love is a banquet for two with the diners graciously passing the various dishes back and forth and sharing them without reserve until they suddenly grab for the dessert like gluttonous children. Egoists turn love into a carnal tug of war but the rope keeps breaking and the contestants tumble backward with bruised souls, like sleepers rudely awakened. In blissfully romantic affairs where neither loves less or more than the other, even the dessert goes down mutually and instead of a tug of war we have a kind of quadrille in which the dancers keep changing places and sex; and in total love woman's body turns into the airplane man rides for that final flight straight up into the clouds.

The stomach nerves set the bell of laughter pealing. These nerves become so wearied when the stomach is too grossly full that laughter simply liquifies. At the end of a banquet the laughter of the guests sounds like a shower of rain splashing down, the sound of a river's suddenly catching its own falling self over rocks and sharp cliffs. The fullest laughter—like bells beaten on and on—comes from fasting.

The harder the earth, the firmer it holds the roots of the trees and the more the branches stretch up and away in order to tear the whole tree loose. Most great minds are bourgeois in origin with their roots in the people.

On the other hand, the branches of a plant that grows on soft and porous ground tend to splay outward rather than upward. Think of all those authors who write only to escape their situation in life.

Red is the liveliest of all colors, yellow is the highest of all tones. Beyond a certain intensity the fire in red actually turns blue; but no matter how intensely yellow flames, it will first consume whatever form it happens to be the color of before it turns into white. Yellow is the flaming sun itself, the fieriest fire, most luminous of all buoys, lighthouse of lighthouses, the X-ray of colors, the hinge of the spectrum, the stem of sunlight in flower, the suspension wire of the Chandelier of All Colors, the main cable that brings light into this world, the chromatic telephone of the Invisible, the loudspeaker of God, the staircase between earth and sky, the topmost stair leading to Eternity.

The filings of white in the light we see are pale blue in color because of the shadows between the white particles. The blue of the sky is the result of white light subdivided by the filing blades of the air.

A thin thread of water comes to drink of a pool and urges the pool forward in flood, itself nourished by the dormant swell beneath the surface, which fed the pool but which would never overflow without the addition of that thin thread—would have remained a pool forever, unknown to distant countrysides. There are so many women of superior intelligence whose remarkable powers are hidden and who die "pools." They stagnate forever because not even the most insignificant heart of a man has ever beaten in unison with theirs for a moment, and yet their hands could have warmed the cold brain of some man to unending exertions, and transformed that thin thread of spiritual water into bounding waves. A little love, and merely that, is all the great minds of women need to make them overflow.

Fat and thin are interrelated and blend in the act of touching under the slightest pressure of the hand, resisting and yet giving way successively or simultaneously. The breast's fullness both envelops and presses against the fingers at the same time as they touch and press it. By the act of enveloping and doubly touching, the breasts are at the same time the ultimate in fatness and thinness according as we perceive by fits and starts that we do the touching or that the breasts are touching our fingers.

Genius has a choice of three exits from life: fame, suicide, or madness. If the door of fame refuses to open, the other two are the only ones left. Otherwise he risks an even worse collapse: having his mind corrode his entire "skeleton" and his body reduced to chalk so that it pays its debt to the world on a hospital bed. Genius has no choice but to risk death. No choice at all: it's either forward march or be utterly burned and consumed in the flesh like the body of Lot's wife turned into a form of mineral life when she glanced behind in the hope of retracing her steps. Most men can resort to women for their way out. To genius woman is a trap. He has to avoid her at all costs or be a nonentity. Woman is harmless for the man of genius only after the advent of fame, after his work is done, the electricity of his effort has been discharged, and the full life of his spirit has been emptied at last. Genius is like water, the genial element in nature, which can be contained or hardened into its own container but which can also shatter the stoutest rocks or crack the hardest metals when it wants to escape.

The bishop's mitre is nothing but the crest of the cockatoo. The guardsman's plumed casque was inspired by the comb of the bird of paradise. Every woman's hat belongs to the same family as the jaunty headfeathers of birds. The difference is that the bishop's mitre conflicts with his stole, the plumed casque breaks the martial rhythm with too strong an accent of its own, and there isn't a woman's hat imaginable that doesn't look "made" for some other woman's head. Human headgear may imitate the coiffure of birds, but our bodies don't move the way theirs do: every little hop a bird takes harmonizes its head-dress with its head. The bird's hat and the bird's clothes are one and the same as they never are with us. The only perfect human head-covering would be a *naked* crest for a naked body. Anything else would look fake, like makeup, a patchwork imitation of the supreme perfection—of what?—of an inferior species.

Grey is the Styx of color, the boundary line between white and black, the frontier of all colors. Colors that die once they have passed the stage of grey disappear into invisibility. Any material that has grey on all sides turns anemic at the edges. Grey suits a loose fit in clothing because it deadens color seen from a distance, and to that extent it is particularly kind to old age, for it keeps the beholder's eye from concentrating on the unflattering advertisement of bodily decrepitude signalled by the bright colors.

We are alive in the smallest of our hair follicles, in all our vertebrae, even in our excrement. But our nails extract from us only a low level of survival because they feed off the waste portions of our blood. Now blood is perhaps the most spiritual part of the entire spirit life led by the body—and the greater the distance between the full flow of our blood and its residues, the more inert is the dross itself, as Lucifer, once the Angel of Light, now survives as the substratum of the kingdom of shades.

We always pump more space into our lungs when our hearts are content. But this pumped-in space has nothing in common with the actual volume of air inhaled, for space is spirit as well as body and qualitatively different from the resiliency or the volume of air absorbed. Think how buoyant every cell in your body feels, how your whole physique expands, and how your spirit seems to float on high whenever you take a deep breath in an exultant mood.

The iceberg is a platform of water. When the coldness of egoism solidifies the soul, it becomes easily penetrable. Egoism is the worst line of defense against the self. The only way to defend ourselves thoroughly against the world is by altruism.

Measure a piece of brightly colored material and notice how you tend to overestimate its size. Bright colors speed up your rate of vision. The axial screw in the compass of your arms is under the control of your color sense. Because their color compass is internal, the blind have no use for our geography of measurement. When a blind man points at the blue of the sky, his arm sketches broadly; he launches his hand into space to touch the soft whiteness of clouds. His gestures are irrelevant to time and they drink up space like a butterfly's wings, as if the whole earth were at their disposal. People whose color sense is weak are somewhat blind in their movements. The color-blind person is a wretched judge of distance and can't tell whether objects are near or far.

Nothing in the realm of taste combines tasting and smelling as well as vinegar. One whiff of vinegar in the salad wafts the whole concoction into your mouth. Your neighbor's tart armpits assailing your nostrils at table puts an edge on your food.

When you dream, your phantom self lies stretched out on the mattress of the pupil fitted to its box-spring iris on the bed of the white of the eye. When the expression of the eye is dormant, the subconscious floats up into full view. To know what people are really like, spy on them when their look lies a-dreaming. Man escapes from the prison of himself only when he is "absent."

All the colors in nature are in good taste. The scenery can be all out of shape, with vegetation battered and contorted by wind and weather, but every color nature wears will still "go" with what she has on.

There is no such thing as absolute flatness because all color is an impasto of form. Touching is inseparable from seeing. Shut your eyes and color will still be there like the head of the Cheshire cat. The eye's sense of touch and the fingers' sense of sight combine to "deform" everything man touches. He experiences the sensation of absolute flatness only in death, when color lies stretched out in the eye and the human sense of touch becomes coextensive with the absolute itself.

All the adjuncts to the mechanics of seeing are integral to our look: eyebrows, eyelashes, eyelids, and the ball of the eye itself can never be dissociated without changing the nature of the look. Plucked eyebrows put a flat roof on our look. The circles of the eyes reduce the look's basement area. False lashes make a tawdry peristyle. And when a new type of cosmetic someday changes the size of the eyesocket, the eye will simply end up in prison. The only genuine making-up for the eye is to enlarge the pupil's breadth of soul and thereby add wings to the house of our spirituality. Eyes are not measurable as large or small but as soulful or empty. Only God can fit out an eye. Without God's help eyes are clownish, phony, or fraudulent.

Foam is the most perfect of all swimmers. The body of foam is so perfectly relaxed that it lets itself be borne by the water without the effort of a slightest gesture. We would be better swimmers if our minds were disengaged. All current swimming records would be broken if we could only teach our athletes to unlearn thinking their movements.

The human glance is a compass perfectly adapted to making measurements but completely useless for drawing circles with, because any line dissolves the moment the adjustable arm of the compass has begun to scribe and the tracing reverts to white paper en route to its destination. The glance in the round is one of God's looks, not man's.

A kiss is two butterflies of flesh mutually gobbling flies against a blue sky tinged purple by their enormous wings, two infinite beings in the same love-sky frantically trying to lose themselves in each other—like light and color mutually counter-straining in a dazzle of sunshine.

Tender feelings impoverish the eyes and enrich the mouth. Anger snuffs the mouth and lights up the eyes.

We use the term "normal" without a clear sense of any human standard of normality. Someone considered normal for his own historical period would never fit the standards of any other time, past or future. Normality is a moral idea measured by the yardstick of manners and politics. The "abnormal" leaders of the governing classes are always in tacit agreement about the need to prevent the common man from scaling the heights of the Establishment. Political, cultural, and financial tyrannies habitually and selfishly see to it that the world stays "normal" so that they themselves can flout standards. The middle classes originated as the incarnation of normality. By glorifying themselves and achieving absolute self-satisfaction they prepared a lovely dung-heap in which dictators might spring up overnight like mushrooms. The more normal people there are as spitting moral images of everybody else, the easier it is for agitators, madmen, and epileptics to seize control of the ship of state and lead whole nations to their ruin.

Although desire is the shortest way to the heart, the ground is uneven, full of steep hills and unexpected gorges. To keep your hopes alive and your strength from failing while still trying to follow the exact route, you have to build bridges across these surprises. Resurgences of feeling inspired by common interests span the gulf of sex.

There is a brilliant sun in every pearl and a glowing moon as well, mingling their beams in one sole flame.... The pearl is the only place on the surface of the earth where sun and moon shine with equal force in the same "sky." The pearl is a nacreous sun and a crystal moon set in a milk bath of silver.

Only children laugh at the doll's face when its rubbery features are squeezed together. But children laugh at anything, their laughter is essentially careless, overbubbling, and innocent. They laugh at themselves in themselves, like all other pure and happy types. We grownups find nothing amusing in the doll's distorted features. We don't see anything human in its death mask of a face. In essence man laughs only at man. If we suddenly came upon an angel with his wings on crooked, not even the ghost of a smile would cross our lips or twinkle in our eyes. No laugh can survive in the extra-human stratospheres of life.

A cake of ice creaks like a metal machine: ice cracking sounds like wood clacking. Water flowing sounds like the wind, fire, or other liquid noises, from animal through vegetable, including the human voice; but the sound made by *solid water* has no connection with anything else in life except the clicking and clanking of the last agony.

Those parts of the skin that are insentient are the blinkers of our sense of touch. The only time we touch with complete abandon—in total awareness—is at the moment of expulsion from the uterus.

The movement of our hips is the most generous of all our bodily movements. There is nothing stingy about hip transactions, no concern with retail or small-lot wholesale selling in the comings and goings along the bust-to-leg exchange. Hip movement is life in action—whether we want to or not, we express ourselves completely in our hips. Think of all the women who vainly try to dissemble what their pelvises do, try to save face so that nobody will know how those great unmasking swivel joints unequivocally translate the soul's deepest meanings into their own frank gestures. The hips are fully themselves only in the action of walking—in the way a heap of gold sparkles when you stir it or the eye lights up in movements. The hips have no inner self except when active. Women's movements are regulated by the beat of their hips' pulses; the sensitiveness of the watch is a function of the elasticity of the watchspring. The hips are the mainspring of the body-clock.

In proportion to the size of the head, a woman's cheeks are measurably larger than a man's, but a man's forehead is just as measurably wider than a woman's. There's always something hip-like about women's faces, they have a naturally "seated" look. There's always something bustlike about the "stance" in men's faces.

No one is closer to you than your own belly. Eating is man's "neighborly" duty. Beyond a certain point fasting is a crime against God more than against Nature—fasting is the human body as dagger turned against the life of the spirit, deliberately foiling God's plans. Prolonged fasting is a worse gesture of rebellion than a savage act of suicide, for suicide by violent means amounts to throwing yourself in front of the wheels of the chariot of life, whereas suicide by fasting bars the chariot's road on its way to God.

The little finger has the range of a magnifying glass, the index finger of an opera glass. Seeking a lost object on the ground, the little finger quivers more nervously than all the others. We use the index to point out a distant scene as if trying to touch it where the eyes can hardly make it out.

Man wants his religion to be above all *comfortable*. Religious intolerance is the sign of religious decline. To fill all the pews, churches have to be easy chairs for the heart and not torture racks for the spirit.

The sun has the right key for opening all the locks of things except the human eye, so soundly immured in its egoism and encased in its own nature that the sun has to use trick keys to let its light in. If it didn't resort to subterfuge, the outside world would simply never get in. The idea may sound far-fetched, but what about that concave, blocked-up look in the miser's eye? Misers little by little convert the living world into such a myth that eventually the only light that ever penetrates is the gleam of their gold.

After puberty the female thumb and fingers still manage to look chaste, all except the little finger. At fifteen see how that little finger wiggles! It responds like a seismograph needle to every quake of desire. Woman drinks with the little finger, and women who really like their pleasures are always sipping from its glass. The ebbing of sexuality in the aged desensitizes the little finger long before the others are affected.

The finger joints are the neutral points of the caress, like the golden links between the beads of the rosary on which prayers glide along uninterruptedly. The caress halts merely an instant at the finger joints as the kiss of the skin stops for breath.

You can't "redo" a picture by putting it in a magnificent frame. What good does it do the face to have a pair of lovely eyes if the soul is empty? The eyes of a truly great man disappear like canvas under masses of glowing colors. His glance is both canvas and frame on the endless wall of his facial expression.

Solitude opens the compass legs of the eye; company closes them again. The inflections of individual voices become less pronounced as the group increases in size. Crowds contract our natures even as we draw in our bodies to let strangers pass.

What distinguishes essence from accident in any man's life is the extent to which his life wobbles on its axis. Now, animals are steeped in essentiality, they live by it since it lies at the center of their nature. Disorient an animal by caging him and he develops perversions, a sidewise way of engaging experience, as the textile of his sensations concerns him less than the trimmings.

All animals dance with joy when they feel happy: some dance with their heads, some with their legs or bust, others with their ears, but most of them with their tails. Their cries of joy are few and far between. Man, however, has buried his animal expressiveness so deep inside him that civilized manners allow him only one outlet for dancing with joy: laughter. But he flings about in laughter only when he feels sure that he won't be laughed at for doing so.

The first sensations of life remain our standard of measurement for the rest of our lives. Hollow, full, long, wide, empty, sharp, rough, smooth, nauseating, sweet, bitter, shrill, heavy, and so forth: these ideas insofar as they become embodied in our minds at infancy reflect our entire manner of apprehending sensations during the rest of life. Sensorially speaking, we are the finished products of the sensory manufacture that began when we were just born. Who can say that the infant in the uterus does not suffer through its mother's senses the sensory shock of the world outside, and that the mother is not, in turn, responsible for certain deformities, certain magnified tics, which leave their mark upon the baby's body forever? Think of all the women who smother their children with care and who must have wearied them to death even in the womb. We now have gynecologists, pediatricians, and specialists in infant surgery. Wait and you will see the medical schools some day train foetal specialists in the attempt to stave off the death of the race from the very beginning of life, so that man may be insured of his bodily welfare even before birth.

The eye drinks and eats in the pupil, chews and digests in the iris, and evacuates its thoughts in the white. Intense curiosity: all the eye becomes its pupil. Faraway look: only the iris is visible.

Emptiness of mind beyond thought and desire: only the white shines in the grey and overcast sky of the look, like the double horns of a silvery moon.

Beyond a certain rate of speed, the idea of air becomes meaningless. In future spaceships, every instant of forward flight will feel like an empty ballooning. Beyond a certain degree of thought as measurement, everything becomes spiritual in our finite brains. That is what space as an idea really means. If you look long and steadily at an object, your sensory grasp of the world relaxes; your eye seems physically no longer there; and your sight passes to another plane of time beyond that measured in terms of light. Now, with a last effort, concentrate your eye even more fixedly, and space dissolves as you pass into the world of spirit. This is what prophets and seers always do, shedding time and space as they launch themselves into the infinite.

In general those who have limited ideas sleep deeply as if to stretch out their stunted thoughts in the vast mold of the subconscious. The proof is evident in imbeciles, who are liveliest in the morning but whose minds progressively deteriorate as day goes on. Imbeciles are very irritating at noon, but most of all at night. Their minds have gone to bed long before they have. Imbeciles yawn more than most people. An intelligent man yawns with his body in his mind, the imbecile with his mind in his body, a little like an animal, whose yawn is a kind of cellular laughter.

The hollow sound of tin: of all metallic sounds the most cavernous, like a Chinese box of booming barks. Add tin instruments to an orchestra, and the brasses, woodwinds, and strings would sound as if they kept poking their heads elastically out of the cave—as if the orchestra were throwing its voice like a ventriloquist. Silver, second cousin to tin, gives a little something of the same effect. The silver flutes we read about in ancient Persian orchestras must have sounded like a voice from another world. And then, think, too, of the supernatural effect attributed to the silver trumpets mentioned in the Bible!

Put an infinite variety of animal faces in superimposition and what you will have is the basic mold of the human countenance without the picture.

Autumn is all the seasons in palimpsest.

God is the only neutral point of ideas (the dead center of a hurricane being its pivotal position) whereas we humans are either a little too much to the right or left of ideas. If we were ever squarely in the middle of any idea at all, our "self-consciousness" would dissolve as we became reabsorbed into the Deity. For God doesn't think, he simply exists. Life doesn't think, it is. Life is the reflex action of the absolute, the quintessence of thought: the center of the hurricane is the dispatching of forces into combat irrespective of general orders. Beyond a certain basic energy, thought dissolves in action. In the crucial moment of battle the commanding general is no longer human but animal, incarnating the peculiar brilliance of the savage beast. The kind of intelligence needed for fighting wars is of course the mind of a cave man: the unbeatable soldier would be a cave man with modern weapons. At the decisive moment of action the true battle commander turns all the thinking over to his body. His mind functions in reflex movements like a moral robot under remote supernatural control. Real military genius at the split seconds of decision is a paper kite swung about by the winds of destiny.

No caress would be secure if the thumb didn't notch it into place. When the thumb takes little part in a caress, touching drifts; without its last word there is no finality. In a handclasp the thumb's assignment is to give the crowning grace.

The tip of the tongue is the antechamber of tasting, like a table set before a meal. The tip of the tongue puts all flavors into separate dishes. Gourmets, those analysts of enjoyment, eat with the tip of the tongue and savor liquids as well. Indeed, the more disagreeable we find a course, the more we relegate it to the back of the mouth. One literally swallows medicine, whether solid or liquid. Food eaten without appetite is quickly bolted, but when the senses are acute one even sips sauces.

Animals rest their glances on things but when they fix their gaze on man they seem to exceed their objective, as in the look of condescension that skims over the head of someone not quite worth acknowledging.

Deep feeling makes the lungs breathe even in the eyes. The eyes are the highest Bridge of Sighs.

Babies laugh with their hands, even down to between their fingers, which repeat the movements of their lips. When a man lies dying, half-divinely deaf and dumb already, his whole face closes shop while his fingers take over the tallying.

The absorbed reader looks asleep. Fixity of attention is the best kind of sleeping pill. When the spirit wakes the body rests. The stiff body of the hypnotised subject. The physical lethargy of fixed ideas. The madman strips flesh and bone down to the naked mind. Ecstasy lays the body on its bier.

Our Earth is most certainly the Moon's moon just as the Moon is our moon. Think of all the people who see us as we see them—but the blinding sun of our egos keeps us hidden from ourselves as the blinding sun of our day keeps the Earth from seeing how the Moon sees it. The blind light of self-love keeps us from seeing what the world thinks of us.

The whole universe lurks in the well of the human eye. The light of certain stars may take thousands of years to reach us but ages elapse before some parts of our eyes' visual experience sink to the subsoil of our memories. We inherit from our ancestors a visual legacy that time can never exhaust. Adam continues to gaze back at Eden through the medium of our eyes, whose ocularity a thousand years from now will serve our descendants as well. What else is theosophy but an unbroken visual chain transcribed and organized as reincarnation, like those ophthalmic disorders that make us see a whole world of things that simply isn't there. Our forebears have not disappeared underground. Just as they continue to throb in our veins so do we believe that before we were committed to our present frames of flesh we must ages ago have occupied some past being's body. Under conditions of extreme fear it is not I who trembles but some unrecognizable phantom Me. And what else is madness but a mental invasion of our privacy? The art of living consists in eliminating all the hereditary crowding in the room of the self. Eradicate the weeds if you want your own seedling to grow. So man's first duty is to rid himself of the unwanted dead in his veins as a dog picks off fleas, as the blood pimple regurgitates its pus. Stripping back to the seedling will reveal the face of God in it just as the time-descending act of love reincarnates the youthful you inside yourself.

Animals make tactile judgments by flicking at the sides of things with their paws. They have no fingers to fondle with, so they tap with their claws. Babies do the same. The child learns to become an adult by diffusing his animality from his hands into his body. The willowy infant stiffens into a man as he grows older while at the same time his sense of touch decoagulates its animality. As children mature they grow human hands but animal bodies.

Man isn't the only being who doffs his hat in greeting. Animals incline their ears and lift their tails a bit when they meet just as men take off their hats and waggle. Man's civilized gestures have their counterparts in animal social codes. With this important difference: we do it irregularly, they do it invariably. Animal politeness is instinctive and unremitting; human politeness is deliberate and occasional. The animal is civilized through and through. Man is a superficially-polite brute at heart.

The one-way direction of the sun's rays from heaven to earth is the only unilateral contract in the laws of the universe. And like the symbolic star of the sun, God is an unconditional life-giver. This means that we can no more abdicate our own immortality than the flower can vomit up its sunlight. There are no suicides in the afterlife. The torture of the damned that suicides suffer in the world beyond is precisely that they have to go on living forever swollen with egotistical hate of their own egos. After all, man commits suicide on earth because he failed to shape the whole wide world to his heart's desire—even as lovers renounce love because they are unable to consume it utterly.

The capitalist wants to be sure his tomb is ready to receive him after he dies, eager to be comfortable even in stone. The capitalistic instinct stays close to the heels of the corpse itself. Egoism harries us even to the tomb. Because we love ourselves so much, if we were ever able to come back to life we would kiss our own graves just as we once cherished our own breath.

Space and time overlap when you walk with your eyes turned to the sky. Time turns into space and space oozes forward the way a galloping horse appropriates the plain while the plain seems to be leaping ahead on its own. After a long period of sky-gazing you develop a sense of infinity well on the far side of all time and space ideas—a sense that compresses emotion into sensation and explains why men have always thought that Heaven was an actual place in the stratosphere.

Fear turns the thumb into the little finger and the little finger into the thumb. Fear destroys all sense of right and left in our arms and legs. Fear makes it impossible to tell which side of us is which. A frightened man tries to look ahead and behind at the same time, his soul tumbling inside his body, like a dancer's spinning head leaping after the wake of her twirling body. Fear makes us do pirouettes inside ourselves, momentarily ending our inner sense of right and left, the way the dancer for one split second after each *entrechat* loses her sense of direction on stage.

The act of love is the only kind of entertainment without intermissions. Lovemaking is always a one-act play no matter how long the performance or how drawn out and complicated the production.

If we knew how to sublimate the act of love through our five senses as we turn the course of a waterflow or tap a stream we would all be gods. Of course, to some small extent the Yogi sublimates his sexuality, although he really doesn't control it at will the way you turn a valve off and on because the same divine grasp that manipulates all life's handles holds the love-act equally fast. The human body squirming in passion is still only an exhaust pipe extending from the world beyond. The water faucet doesn't "own" the water in the tank, it conducts it, and so we who think we possess some woman are merely possessed by the act of love, by a spiritual lightning bolt travelling through the electrode of our being. Woman serves as the ground for carnal electrocution.

An intense shade of blue sends out grey streamers. Deep blue skies make the clouds look smoky. Any little trace of blue on grey material intensifies the general color. Bluish grey of the flesh around turquoise. Lapis-lazuli miscegenates with the skin. The bluish iris of the sea monochromes the features in grey. Turquoise spouts opalescent reflections at noon.

What could exercise our sense of touch more completely than the flat of the hand—and yet even when it makes the widest possible surface contact with anything it still may not feel the object's or body's *nearness* at all points. The same is true for all kinds of touching, not only the palm's. The absolute authority of the sensation of touching is one thing but the sensation of nearness or farness is another—no matter how crushed together any two human bodies may be. Think of bodies that have clasped you with suffocating closeness: weren't some of them paradoxically a million miles away? Think of arms that have embraced you tightly while paradoxically holding you at arms' length. Think of all the pure biological copulation that takes place between—so to speak—two embankments connected by a thin thread of land. The feeling of physical conjunction in our sense of touch derives from and varies greatly according to our body's psychic zones. *Near* and *far* are equally states of soul as they are physical sensations and the conditions of bodily response. Love adds another dimension to our physical state of being.

Look into a man's eyes if you want to know how his health has been, look at his hair to see how well he is now, and "read" his lips to see how he survives. The mouth has been plunged more deeply into the waters of the future than any of his other features. His eyes will never predict a thing. God spoke and man became flesh, and since then the mouth has been the soul's forestage. The Word is the scout for the main body of worlds behind and other worlds to follow. Christ's words prepare our way to Eternity, for his mouth is in the Father while his transfiguring flesh becomes the mystic body of churches: a tremendous floating bridge between the worlds of matter and spirit.

The thumb is the Trojan Horse of our sense of touch: it contorts itself as if trying to conceal its movements before attacking, like an Oriental making deep bows to keep his quick glances hidden.

The smell of fruit and the smell of flowers are degrees on the same compass of odors. The fruit smell of our body joints, the flower smell of our skin, are products of the same sudation of blood. The only sexual difference is that male odors thrust out at you, female odors fan out at you.

Fear binds our sense of smell. A human being in deep distress gropes with his nose.

Ages ago when men were exclusively instinctive creatures, they were all equally intelligent. because every single being was in touch with everything there was to know. The only mark of distinction will have been some more or less lofty conception of God. Then, as his instincts began to atrophy, man had to develop the capacity to learn. The last of his natural responses took refuge in Faith, or the instinctive grasp of God. Those whose dregs of instinct lacked any taste of God resorted to additives; those too asthmatic to take one last gulp of the divine needed pulmonation. They used fetishes for road rests, superstitions for way stations on the unfamiliar journey. Idolatry and demonism are homeopathic doses of omnipotence, falsified and perverted notions of God that men lick up in droplets. An authentic idea of God would have suffocated them in the way too strong a drug can poison an enfeebled patient. Fetishes, statues, and idols are abcesses formed by spiritual pus: if men had bypassed God by believing exclusively in matter, their souls would have dropped off with gangrene. Doubting Thomas had to touch Christ's wounds; we have to package God, harden his image into clay. Let a few millennia pass, however, and the primary significance of iconism will fade. We may then have to touch God's flesh and bone to believe. Now, since for a materialist the only tangible thing about God is his power, men will eventually try to materialize him through nuclear fission, by forcing him out of a trap door like Mephistofeles in *Faust*. Our distant descendants will have given up invocation through images to force God into view by making Him backtrack like a difting boat that you wash to the bank by scooping water towards you. At this stage fetish as force will replace fetish as thing, prayer will become coercion. Man's instinctual perception of God will have passed through the visual intermediary point of fetishism to reach the last stage: forcible entry. The child baffled by his dog's gesture language twists its tail to make it speak. The toying at seduction that we still practice in idolatry today will end in the twilight days of the human species as the rape of God. The man whose words go up while his thoughts lie here below when he calls upon or supplicates his God is trying to coerce him, trying to violate God's own freedom.

The smell of the rose is heaven itself, while the smell of the pink is a Jacob's ladder connecting the two poles of fragrance, human and angelic, stinging and smooth. The rose may be more "divine" but the pink is more divinely human. The pink's smell is endlessly self-replenishing, each wave of fragrance that pulsates from it surprises us—like certain exquisite mouths whose breath is different each time their burning lips tremble. It is as if mere frailty could mother an immortal soul. The rose is more of a spiritual stimulant, the pink is more of a bracing tonic. In times of trouble a little self-indulgence is worth more than a sermon.

Nobody dies wide awake spiritually. We all leave life in a drugged state of soul, so that the newly fleshed spirit may never use his port of exit as a port of re-entry—and so that the damned don't swarm back to earth.

The curvature of the loins "anticipates" the modelling of the breasts. The bend of the hips is an enlarged tracing of the droop of the shoulders. All the flaring lines of the human physique are harmonically related and individually characteristic of each body. Without uniqueness in its system of enlarging curves there would be no feeling of unity to the human body, whose patchwork of forms would tend to swallow up the individuality of each physical movement.

The loveliest parts of the foamy tissue of lace are its openings. The thrill of a spoken compliment lies in the pauses. The heart feeds on silence more than on anything else.

One's instinct for sexual pleasure is virginal even when one's sex is not. The lowest gutter whore starts every new copulation from scratch. The hidden heart of sex is incorruptible because the love act is the most precious and perfect of God's gifts. If sex weren't source-pure, how could we reproduce our own image?

Water flows in a running brook like a comb combing its own teeth. Microscopic analysis of running water shows a superimposition of "combs," layer after layer trying to rake its own filaments out straight. Flowing is water's way of resuming its main purpose while rugged banks and uneven river bed interrupt its coursing and disturb the smoothness of its motion. Flowing is water's way of assigning its manpower to units and marshalling its forces. Any gush of water is a harnessed volcano: the highest form of maintenance. The next time you decide to set your ideas in order, follow some trickling stream along.

Animals have serious faces when they play; their bodies do their laughing for them. With humans it's just the opposite: our gestures become stiff and shapeless and "animalistic" as laughter invades our features. The ecstasy of guffawing drains everything human from the body until it waddles like an ape or flumps like an elephant pawing, the ape's arms beating like clumsy chicken wings, the elephant's loins trembling as if with equine snorts. Laughter is natural to man, but nothing reduces the body to bestiality more than this unique gift of laughter. Only the progressive refinement of the spirit escapes such degradation, the smile outlasting the laugh, the laugh angelically becoming a smile. Devils howl stridently with laughter; angels are resonant and bell-like.

The earth isn't the only naturally attracting force around us: every object in the world emits waves peculiar to its kind and to the disposition of its particles of matter. The atom being a system of electrical charges, all objects would seem to be shortwave micro-stations sending out messages in wave lengths determined by their surface features. This is what we mean by an object's "ambiance," or the way wireless emissions of the furniture of a room affect us. Rearrange the pieces and we respond to them differently.

Matter is classified as solid, gas, and liquid—a division based on the sharpness of our sight and the penetration of our sense of touch. Birds perceive the world differently; to them liquid is a moving solid and all solids are more or less as hard as steel. Their sense of touch depends on the delicate airborne flow of their own gestures. The fish in his half-solid element—the hard liquid of wave and current—sees air as a vacuum and solid as a plastic. If man had been born to air as he was to earth, gas and liquid would seem different degrees of solid to him. We have "cut up" matter into three parts, evaluating them according to their different capacities for remaining erect: solid on its legs, liquid sitting down, and gas prostrate. All forms of life on earth would feel hard to the airy palpation of an angel's finger. Seen from above, the three arbitrary classifications of solid, liquid, and gas would appear like one undifferentiated block of matter. Nature is malleable to the senses, as any sick man can attest, for his sense of touch has begun to decoagulate and his sense of sight to turn doughy; his hands slide over hard objects as if they were resilient, and every hard object changes into soft clay, all surrounding nature into a muddy liquid. Objects flow between the sick man's fingers, yet his weary lungs seem to be breathing solids. Animals simply do not have our idea of solid, liquid, and gas: their senses lead them to other conclusions. People from Mars, Jupiter, the Earth, and the Moon must have altogether different physical conceptions of matter. Each one biologically assimilates his world in his own way. Our ambiance is more or less tough to the bite of our senses according to the length of their teeth.

Blue adheres tenuously to the forms of things. It makes poor drapery for any but the firmest flesh and doesn't suit hesitant gestures. It is the ideal color for "military" frames severe in every movement. Blue at the furling end of a flag makes the other colors cascade.

The equivalent of living *on* the Earth will someday be living *in* the moon: the divergence in the manner of speaking expresses the nature of seeing. Both worlds are round, but our eyes tend to conceive of distant objects as concave because we *rest* our sight on nearby things while we *put* out sight into distant things like a marble in a bowl. Things up close we pick apart one by one, things at a distance we ransack; the vaster the spaces in between, the more desperately does the eye look for something substantial to settle its gaze on. The eye bores into the starry vault of night like a gimlet, drilling each star that draws our glance.

Yellow in the background elongates all surrounding shades. Nothing flattens out a face like a towhead.

The sun's slowest reflexes are the shadows it makes. Shadows are restless light echoes whose rate of travel depends on the air's lubricity and the smoothness of surfaces. Shadows run on the plains, walk in valleys, gallop in summer, and trot in winter.

The dying mouth is recognizable by the white piping around its borders. The flower's last agony shows up as an opaline tint around its mouth. The mouth: the first part of the face that death sets its seal on. When the mouth drains, white and bloodless lips withdraw into a pale emptiness like a discolored corpse lying in lime—the end is not far off.

A stable object and the space it occupies become a part of our visual expectation. Remove the object and its emptied space blinds us: the object being no longer there to fill our sight, its psychic death floods the place from which the carcase disappeared. And whenever some human person leaves this world, the husk of space he once occupied strikes us blind because it was his unique mind that gave consistency to the world around him. Not being permitted to see him anymore, we become incapable of visualizing those things once invested by his spirit, for the only object that filled our own *spiritual space* was his presence.

Cascading water convulses the surrounding air. Listen to the music of any orchestra and every now and then you will hear chaos. The jumblings of water in the waterfall intensify the brilliance of its power and the symphony of its twinklings. The spiritual force of Wagnerian music stems from its inner chaos. The deep psychic center of painting is the chromatic turbulence where colors impinge on each other: the eye recoils, confused by a ubiquity of colors unable to find their places. Music has to disorient the ear, painting has to bewilder our psychic perception of color, if they hope to engage the spirit as well as the senses.

All words ring hollow in a well of silence. To win in argument confuse your opponent by letting his words drop into a void. Indifference is the cyclonic void that can snap and twist words like columns of air. Silence is your champion against evil. If you oppose evil with words, it will cross them like a bridge to penetrate your soul: so blow it up instead by laying your words like sticks of dynamite in the cracks of its silences. Arm yourself with silence, the supreme sword of justice. Words wound, silence kills.

Light clings to silk in flashing folds without ever stretching the material. In contrast, velvet makes light elastic. Silk makes the belly undulate; velvet makes the haunches balloon where there is least play of skin. The tighter the velvet, the plumper a woman looks. Silk makes a dress serpentine. Silk on a thin frame changes what was a slender body into a dancing snake.

In the dark our lips make use of our teeth to seek out another's mouth, just as at night our arm relies partially on its elbow for a helping hand to brush aside each item of blackness. In the dark of night our teeth tiptoe to the kiss upon the carpet of our lips, the two mouths on mutual "all fours." Infantile kisses of benighted mouths. Gestures steeped in the alembic of night. Night insures innocence—night where so many of the dead lie down and so many of the living are born.

A candle flame is a watery jet of triangular fire. All artificial flames end in a needle point. Natural flame is a scarf furling and unfurling. Wherever it interferes, man's hand geometrizes nature.

The eyelashes are the last of the features to grow old in man. Completely white eyelashes would deactivate the glance, and the eye itself would seem buried in the face, just as the landscape seems to go underground after a snowfall. Only the mountain range of the nose would emerge in the heights of the face, an Alp in the naked plains and featureless skies of the forehead.

Apart from the eye—the throne of seeing—no part of the body is any more noble than ignoble: all of its aspects look good in themselves, whether it is chewing or excreting, digesting or eliminating, manufacturing or storing, discharging semen or urinating. Only perversions of function demean it. Constipation deforms the act of defecating. Toothless gums make a cripple of the mouth. Passing water haltingly contorts the limbs. We should keep these images of bodily functions in mind and not pervert our own profession or trade by supposing it to be more ignoble than anyone else's. Otherwise the physical actions we perform while at work may lose their fluency and our own souls take on the servile air of one who sells his dignity for a few measly pennies.

Artists drink color to spew out form. They reshape color in the matrix of their senses. An artist can only work with as much form as his own sense of form accepts. In other words, being his own color block, he works with color by chipping away the marble of his own being.

Teeth turn into furniture in a lifeless face. In the fleshless faces of great spirits, the teeth themselves become spiritualized and develop a kind of facial mobility, a multiple face in the face, integrating themselves with all the features, as bare rock mingles with the foam splashing on it and the face of the waves. When the teeth lose all hope of leaping out of the face, the face is dead. We all know those gloriously brilliant sets of teeth which are like slag in the depths of the expression because the face has no soul. Soul gone from the face is a massacre of the features, the teeth being the first spiritual soldiers to fall, just as the most drill-proud regiments in the army are mowed down first as they walk upright into the cannonade. The teeth are like pearls quickened and set into motion by the spirituality of the skin. Lack of soul snuffs the vestal fires of the teeth just as the absence of spirituality carbonizes the pupil.

The mind's eye is unbelievably supple. If the mind of man could become one with the sun of the atom, this "eye" would behold the stellar-planetary system with the same sense of wonder, magnitude, and limitless awe as the eyes in his head stand amazed before the cloud-capped palaces of the sky. In the realm of spirit, great and small are meaningless terms; spirit creates and recreates the world according to the measure of the soul. God has invested nature with infinity, but our eyes lack the suppleness to see it.

Consider the goat's bearded face: what could be more openhearted if not simple-minded? Lengthen the jaw on a human face and after a certain point it looks a bit moronic. Put a goatee on it and what was mere stupidity begins to seem softly ingenuous. Given the same facial expression, animals always look more spiritual than we do. The Bible uses the paschal lamb to emphasize Christ's spiritual nature. Think of all the animals that are the picture of angels. The Gospels picture the Holy Spirit as a dove, and since Christ entered Jerusalem on an ass rather than a horse, we might reconsider our conventional caricature of that ignominious beast. Someday we may even deify the ass, if we ever come to understand his absolute stubbornness, his categorical nay-saying. Is there any moral decision greater than the ass's "refusal," whose NO!, signifying the mystic redemption of Hell, ought to be engraved on all church porches and cut into the casements of the tabernacle itself.

All the stages of touching are transparent copies of the act of love and follow its basic rhythm: there is a touch of taste, a touch of sight, a touch of smell, a touch of hearing. All the forms of sensation are patterns of the act of love. It is the universal experimental laboratory of all the senses. Doctors would find it more worth their while to confess the "sins" of the bed than those of the body.

The forehead is a flat elastic band stretched out in length by joy and shrunk by fear, widened in height by astonishment and narrowed in curiosity. Indifference diagonalizes the expression of the forehead. The forehead of the man who doesn't care seems neither long nor wide, round nor arched, fat nor thin—nothing but a flat knee in place of a brow. Indifference denatures the forehead, disorganizes and unhinges its dimensions as a listless sky turns a pond into a basin of water whose banks flow and reflow into the water itself, no longer defined by the extent of the colorless and lifeless fluid.

The human voice is a dictionary of sounds. But its pages riffle and flutter as soon as heard. Death alone turns over each page of the voice, one by one. The dying man spells out his sounds as the child his A B C's. Ecstasy—that other form of death—makes unified noises into a chaplet of sounds, so that each voice becomes a vocal piano whose timbres leap across its tones like the percussions that bridge the white and black notes on the pillars of the fingers.

The pace of the snail is made up of thousands of hurried steps, each cell of his immense flat foot acting like a leg proceeding from that knee of a shell he has. So, in spite of the microscopic progress of an infinity of tiny steps, what makes his movement visible is each cellular leg rapidly racing to overtake by displacement each microscopic step ahead. So, too, does man achieve his Paradise, freeing himself from the world and finding his Self again, not by historic and heroic actions but in a thousand tiny selfless minutes flashing with gestures that occupy each second and make the hours go by. The snail, that ticking beast, fills the minute with more seconds than the most violent pistol shot, winning the cross-country race on the track for fifty-yard dashes, making his world tour in a garden plot. Whoever is not afraid of the second lives a thousand lives. The glance of a flower encompasses the universe.

The noise of water is sound riding horse on sound. The noise of wind is a marching infantry of sound. So: the water's thundering hooves and the hurricane's relentless tramp.

Garnet is the apoplexy of mauve. Purple is the embolism of blue.

Lovemaking almost never hits a bullseye. We aim badly and squeeze the trigger always a little off tempo, one eye on ourselves shooting instead of both on the target. We think too much about what we feel, we are too much ourselves ever to be unself-ish.

Elbows are our sidelong direction snobs: more right than right itself, more left than left—*psychic* scouts on reconnaissance. We elbow off the unwanted others who crowd ahead with us just as we walk shoulder to shoulder with our friends, calling them closer with the mystic loudspeakers of our upper bodies. The elbow is a physiological, psychological, and spiritual warning edge.

Still water is the prisoner of its container, running water is the prisoner of its source of movement. Water is free at last only in rain—when the wind keeps its distance—and in the toppling fall of the fountain. And so with us, who are never really free of women except at orgasm and a few moments afterward. Living makes us our own prisoners. Dead, we belong to others. The only real freedom, then, is to drown and sink briefly in our selves.

Here come two of you out of the forest where only the single you entered—as if the experience of entering had engendered a split in your wholeness. This, at least, is how you see and feel yourself, isn't it? Even when absolutely alone, one emerges twice over. I plunge into space single, totally convinced of my physical unity, and yet I rise from its waters a twosome. The child doesn't *see itself* being born, but the man *sees himself* die. It is I and simply I who dives into orgasm to float upward exhausted in my own company. Going to sleep alone, I wake up next to myself. Tasting has one effect, disgust splits and doubles it. And so on with all beginnings and endings.

The throat broadcasts the voice in capitals, the lips in lower case. We speak with our lips to explain, but our throats to persuade.

No matter how much leaves are fixed face to face they always look at each other aslant, whereas all fruits end up head-on however carelessly jumbled. A bunch of flowers is a house of colored cards. A heap of fruit is a hive of colored bees.

Where the ship's prow penetrates the womb of the sea like a plough furrowing the earth, the billows have weeping breasts, the sea swell has watery teats that the wind drinks from drop by drop and the foam laps. The ocean responds sexually to the sexual movements of the vessel like an ardent woman to the touch.

Raindrops sparkling in bright sunshine are candles in the chandelier of the light's rays. Rain in bright sunshine is a fall of fire, droplets of light trickling down like the candle's tears catching fire as they drip.

A tinkling crystal sounds like water turned metallic, like water echoing off a sheet of zinc or any other resonant metal. If water could clack its tongue the sound would be crystalline. All shivering-toned metals produce the same effect. The "veering" tones of the brasses are the purest of all orchestral tones. The brasses are at their best when the orchestration reaches a turning point and the crystalline notes stick out like sharp stalks in the sheaf of gathering sound. The dancer makes her gyrations sing in the same way when her balancing form overflows its own borders like a vase pouring its sides as well as its contents.

Touching flesh causes it to recoil and then fill itself out again to its own shape, the provocation of touch being followed by an act of withdrawal as the flesh tries to desensitize itself. Yet not so much desensitize as auto-sensitize, willfully taking up the sensation given. It is really an incited sensation such as we find among those intense narcissists we call hysterics and those queens of self-concern we call women. This activity—auto-sensation of the self—is perhaps fundamental to the greatest delight we ever receive from our sense of touch. The act of love is the most brilliant example. In love—the auto-palpation of the absolute—women start us off and we run the rest of the race alone. All the great orgies of the flesh such as ecstasy are lonely carousals. All the delights we can imagine end in spiritual masturbation. Self-enjoyment is the end of all delight. Happiness shared is still a separate transport of joy for both. Nirvana is never shared. Beyond a certain form of expression of joy, God is our only companion. Solitude is the condition as well as the ransom of supreme Joy: at those heights the Fire is so intense that living things run the risk of being amalgamated. We can join ourselves forever only to God without the risk of fusion. To become godlike is to become more and more alone *with* one's Joy. The egoist enjoys a lonely joy; the saints are hermits of Joy.

A length of twine is made up of threads interwoven each with all the others separately. Human society contains the same composition and arrangement of wants twisted around together, with each member trying to pull the others his way. It seems obvious that the more complex the intertwining, the tighter the tangle of egos, the easier it will be for some leader to handle. The best twine for knotting and tying is the kind with tightly packed strands.

Foam swims with its fingers. Airy-tentacled, foam is a cuttlefish on the surface of the sea. We all know what it is like to plunge our hands into foam, thousands of little feelers clutching us like the arms of an octopus. A giant spider of water lying in wait to embrace its liquid-fast prey, foam is the sweeper of streams and the brusher of lakes.

In plants, the wrist is merely the hinge of a leaf. In animals, the wrist is liquid, a ligament between the movements of arm and hand, not a joint in itself so much as a mutual extension of both. Only in man does the wrist become instantaneously hard and soft at will, as any gesture requires it: solid or liquid, tense or relaxed in a flash, ready to square the circle in one movement, flying or creeping on call, pawing or plodding, sometimes as peasant-like as the knee, and at other times as aristocratic as the little finger, connecting the neck's spherical movements with the shoulder joint's corkscrew gestures, uniting all finger actions in its microscopic movements and equally enlarging the sheaf of articulations all the fingers are individually capable of. The wrist is master of every expansive modulation contained in the pelvis, every shrinking gesture of the loins. It is the greatest crossroads of human gesture. The entire human body presides over and talks deaf-and-dumb language in the wrist's apparently soothing movements, for which finger and hand get all the credit and reward. The secret of the administrative acuity, the exact source of all this digital cleverness, the essential virtuosity we recognize in painter, sculptor, pianist, and goldsmith, the secret of the hand's entire ability, consists in one thing: making the wrist's power and adroitness flow into the articulation of the finger, making every finger joint a surrogate wrist, delegating some of the wrist's authority to the shoulders, so that every microscopic gesture in the smallest trick of the little finger becomes an exhibition of the entire body's force and character rather than a provincial gesture. In this way the brain does not need to "go through channels" of command and the soul can make immediate contact with life, freeing its spirituality by means of the wrist, which would otherwise be an isthmus of rather elastic flesh across which troops of gesture pass with vacant faces and anesthetic bodies.

There are many women for whom falling in love is a kind of idle toying with themselves as dolls in romantic masturbation. Keep a sharp eye out for the female dying to give herself to you: she may be fondling a plastic heart because her own feelings bore her. The passing breeze of her boredom will evaporate her eagerness as her eyes wander off in search of some other make-believe bottle to feed her doll of a heart with. The ego-swollen heart of the spiritual prostitute with ultrapure flesh has no room in it for any real believing.

Animals in love make every movement and gesture count as a kiss. Before the Expulsion, Adam and Eve couldn't possibly have matched so local a means as kissing to the vast unending field of their Edenic selves.

Impossible to tell where and how fruit looks back at you. Even a fruit whose shape has the most confirmed character can't tell you where to draw its eyes.

Fruit, egg, and light-flash have instantly total fields of vision, they are all-look, their seeing is flush with their being. Fruit, egg, and light-flash telescope into time. Glance at the fruit on its branch, the egg lying about in the farmyard, the dazzle over your shoulder: they have been calmly looking at you already. Your surprise is their awareness, like a hole yawning for your step to stumble into it or a stranger's eye that catches you off guard when you thought you were exploring the psychological moment of seeing without being seen.

Water was made to fall, run, rush out, be suspended or carried, or even leap right through itself—and at the other extreme tiptoe its dewy way along the surface of a leaf. But water's uneasy sense of balance gives it fits of terror and nausea. Giddiness overtakes the fountain at the height of its trajectory so that it never really regains consciousness until it touches ground. Water is the model of all those who try to live two lives at once: sooner or later they fall into a trance and regain their "balance" only when they "land."

The play of shadows on the face of a flower makes it look as if the upper lid of the flower's eye of color is depressed while its lower lid is half-closed—somewhat like a woman who cocks the corner of her hat flirtatiously over one eye. The thrill comes from the two lids never quite meeting at the same level.

Hips and breasts are all of a piece in woman. The movements of a woman's breasts originate in her hips. A full movement of her lower frame makes her breasts dance. When her hips seem most indecisive, her breasts merely sidle along. Torpid hips give rise to the softest motion of the bosom. A wheeling of the hips: the breasts pepper space.

The egoist is like a leech that dies shortly after battening on blood. He has experienced a thousand deaths as a result of his apoplexies of bliss. His misfortune is not to know what to do with his excesses of joy.

Meditation is simply a matter of the ear's refusing to listen and the skin's absorbing silence.

When we cry out in joy, our voices combine with those of our nearest ancestors. When we cry out in fear, our voices sink even farther into the well of time and heredity, resuming the voices of our most distant ancestors the more we tremble with anguish. Fear unrolls the carpet of gestures farther into the past. Extreme terror gives us back something of the gestures of our childhood. A panic-stricken crowd acts infantile, reduced to the helplessness of that time of life when all human gestures most resemble each other.

The index finger is in complete charge of the other fingers when the hand "swims" towards an object—like the admiral's flagship leading the squadron. And the little finger acts as the commanding general whenever the hand grips or seizes something. As soon as the hand strikes out as a fist, the thumb takes over: boxers' thumbs are their most intelligent fingers. The ring finger is the animating spirit of all intertwining, supple and continuous, gestures, as in knitting, sewing, and rocking a cradle. And the middle finger dominates all the unconscious movements of the hand, when the mind is somewhere else. Command and initiative pass in turn from one finger to another as the whole hand requires for any of the intelligent demands it makes on its fingers at a particular moment. The concerted actions of the fingers rely on minds of differing capacities located each in a different member of the hand, just as the human body is made up of an infinite variety of its own intelligent zones.

From the Preface to Volume I of the Mauritian edition of *Sens-Plastique*, reprinted in *Sens-Plastique: Tome II* (Port Louis, Ile Maurice, The General Printing and Stationery Co., Ltd., 1947).

My philosophical position in this work derives from the principle that man and nature are entirely continuous and that all parts of the human body and all expressions of the human face, including their feelings, can actually be discerned in plants, flowers, and fruits, and to an even greater extent in our other selves, animals. And although minerals are usually considered inanimate, death-like rather than life-life, I would have them also tend towards that supreme synthesis, the human form, especially when they are in motion. "Man was made in the image of God," but beyond that I declare that "Nature was made in the image of man." And I hope to prove it.

But I could never have done this by reasoning. I had to rely on subconscious thinking, the only intuitive resource available to humans—which few of us ever use in an entire lifetime. Now, what people mean by the sixth sense is only what I call the hyperactive subconscious, the faculty that enables us to sweep through the darkness of our ignorance with all five senses fanned out at the tips and unified at the base. I should add that I could never have learned to think subconsciously without years of ascetic withdrawal, depriving my body, isolating my self, concentrating my mind and spirit...until by stages I had perfected what I consider to be a totally new method of writing.

* * *

My procedure consisted, first of all, of putting man back into nature by discovering the human face and body in all forms of life. Poets, of course, have always done this; but esthetic intentions are hardly systematic. My purpose was philosophical: to discover what nobody knew rather than to describe what was already there or to make it beautiful.

Second, I put nature back into man's face and body, transmuting whatever is partly or wholly human into active symbols of all forms of life other than human forms.

Third, I mold each feature of the human face to every other one, making them fit and modify each other. If you touch the ends of live wires together, the sparks fly: I make the features take part in lively exchanges.

Fourth, I show the connections between the upper and lower parts of the body, from the chin up and the neck down, according to my axiom: "The human body is an elongated face."

Fifth, I examine each sense by means of every other one along their underground connections, until they actively symbolize each other, my abstractions turn concrete, and my conflicting meanings are resolved.

What could I possibly call this new synthetic way of understanding nature and viewing life? My mode of perception was so personal that I searched for a neologism, but I simply couldn't find one that was accurate and expressive enough. After all, what I had managed to do was to seize humanity and nature with the claws of a pair of pincers, one arm being the five senses, the other my sixth sense; then I scrutinized the senses themselves, two at a time, using the sixth sense as a lens. I finally settled on *sensplastique* because apart from the fact that it seems to say that everything on earth is sensuously connected to everything else and that we all belong to the same mold, "plastic" suggests art in all its forms. I liked that because I consider my whole enterprise to be more of a picture than a book.

22 April, 1945

From the Preface to Volume II of the Mauritian edition of *Sens-Plastique*.

* * *

In *Sens-Plastique* I use a method of analysis based on subdividing my perceptions and impressions to achieve total unity.... That is, I make every part of the human form a symbol of every other part, putting each into each until their individuality fans out into infinity and each part becomes an image of all the others together.... Everywhere I turn I then see in the unity of nature an immanent reflection of the face of God.

* * *

My discovery of a complete *homunculus* in every single part and organ of the human body suddenly made clear to me the allegory of Eve's birth from Adam's rib. I then began to understand that just as the mystical body of God exists in all parts of his creation, so all of man is present in every single part of the human form. Man exists completely in his toe, his neck, and his arms, just as much as he does in his brain, for the soul is "located" everywhere.... The "heart" is no more the exclusive property of a coronary organ than the mind is of a cranium.

* * *

Real sensory introspection would be incomplete and ineffective if it were unable to explain the two greatest sensory phenomena of existence, birth and death. But how can we ever live through birth again knowingly and how can we ever reveal the truth about death without surviving it? The answer lies in an experience available to everyone, the death-birth moment of climax in the act of love. Pornography and sentimentality have always over-intellectualized and exaggerated it as a thing apart, but I make it fit into life as the crossroads of the senses, the mind, the heart, and the soul, a time and place in one, where life and death pass into each other and we pass into ourselves.

April, 1946

From the Afterword to *Sens-Plastique* (Paris: Gallimard, 1948), originally published in *Sens-Plastique: Tome II* (Port Louis, Ile Maurice: The General Printing and Stationery Company, Ltd., 1947).

From the beginning of my literary career I was predisposed to analytical thinking as the result of a combination of factors: my scientific education, a mind trained to think rationally and logically, certain jarring elements in my heredity, and a reserved temperament going back to infancy. For years I sought to dissect man as matter with the abandon of a child taking apart a toy to see how it works. I learned a great deal...but, like most people, more through patience than intelligence.

* * *

That describes the type of thinking characteristic of my first few books. With the fifth volume of my *Pensées* I began to develop another method. It was becoming clear to me that each thing I contemplated, each detail of the human face or body, no matter how insignificant in itself, somehow prompted my imagination, opened up new possibilities of knowledge, quickened the pace of my thinking, led me to the center of the target. I discovered that my mind was beginning to work with lightning accuracy.... Water flowing from a fountain led me to understand something new about space in the universe. If I stared at the swaying of a woman's body, I was suddenly inspired by a metaphysical idea of time.

* * *

I was obviously going in the right direction but still staying too close to the ground, proceeding on too low and level a plane of thought.

* * *

I only began to make decisive progress after I had set myself the task of analysing the human face in depth, and as soon as I did so I saw that all the parts of the face were unavoidably connected with and fit into each other. Intuitively I soon began to see how to understand the features by bridging them and by viewing the human face *in itself* as if I were gazing at a screen inside the face. I now had to avoid being distracted by any actual human faces I knew, to contemplate only what was universally human in itself, and thereby to draw together two facial features at a time, associating them closely enough to extract their essence as if I were squeezing an orange or kneading a lump of rubber to test its quality.

My *literary impressionism by subdivision*...opened up the face to spiritual scrutiny. I next applied the same principle to my observations of the natural world, sensationally kneading each natural form in turn. And in this way I pressed myself into every flower, fruit, and tree, and then folded my integrated self into my primary self, arriving at the same startling results. To put it another way, I forced all objects and things in my experience to yield their secrets to the pressure applied by the pincers of my double self.

I was *photographing from inside* the mind, taking pictures of the human face and the whole world of appearances; but it was stop motion photography in fixed exposures.

I now wanted to *film the mind from the inside*. What I proceeded to do was project a series of pictures on the inside of my mind, subconsciously project on the screen of the conscious mind continuous images of imaginary faces or the real faces of unknown persons drawn from the depths of the subconscious. I showed them at high speed, each "film" consisting of a single face superimposed on an infinite number of still shots of itself. It was the fluency of a single facial "expression" in its infinity of phases looked at in dissociated "takes." I would stop the projector to separate a "take" and then write about it, having seen the essence of the expression in its inmost form.... When I tried to extend interior filming into the natural world I had to rely on exterior observation. This meant—and I only gradually became aware of it—that I now needed to combine the *double vision of my retrogressive narcissism* (integrating my self into the world of things) with *filming the inside of the mind*. The result of the combination, of compressing and uniting the two methods together, was *a triple vision* of man and nature.

* * *

It works like this. First I contemplate the object at hand—a flower, for example—just the way anyone else would view it: in actual vision. Then I integrate it into my self by dividing myself into the flower's world so that the flower "sees me" in return. Obviously this is only an apparent act of seeing by the flower: what really happens is that the separate parts of the double self contemplate each other by means of the flower. Finally...with my *gaze hypnotically attached* to what it sees, I *draw the flower down into my subconscious* (sensationally speaking, by smelling it deeply) until the flower becomes *incarnate* there. At this point the cerebellum projects the flower on the interior screen of my conscious mind where the psychic film unrolls, and the constantly observant mind stops the imagery in flight here and there to extract a still shot and proceeds to write about it.

* * *

From this point on...my mind became so attuned to humanizing nature that I found myself doing so by reflex action. Air, water, the play of light and color, the glitter of light on a leaf, a distant sound, a falling insect, a twig rustling—the least barely material evidence of life other than mine was enough to transform me.... But the real radical change in my thinking was that I stopped treating nature as the *object of my perceptions;* instead, it became the *subject* itself, and not only of my perceptions but of my thoughts. I was *thinking through* and *by means of* life exterior to my own rather than thinking *of* it or *about* it. The exterior world was turning into my own psychic substance as I wove the design of my selfhood into its fabric.... I was no longer thinking. I was letting myself be thought.

* * * *

This reverse action seemed to create a reversion in the actual workings of my mind, as if my brain were being turned inside out. In time I became used to the feeling. It was as though I now dealt with all ideas from within themselves, from their center to their surface: an indication that I had begun sinking into my own subconscious mind in a releasing action that tripped the switch of my sixth sense so that all my latent powers of perception—those profoundly intuitive gifts I least suspected in myself—came to my aid. My ego and my surroundings became each other and I was at the stage of living the environment totally by inner means....

* * *

How can I tell where my mind will take me next? I can only say...that the difficulty of co-ordinating ideas matters much less at this stage than finding the right words to state them in. If I resort from now on to a darkly hermetic language....I will simply have to depend on readers of comparable mind, no matter how few. The trouble in this rarified atmosphere is going to be how to shape and reshape words into a receptacle deep enough to contain these enormous forms of subconscious perception.

I might as well be at the sea's end, plunging my arm into the fine, dry sand and then holding up a handful of siftings: all I need to do is turn my head away for an instant and I know my hand will be empty, for my fingers were never quick enough to keep the grains from slipping away. And so my problem is that language provides a vase neither deep enough to contain nor impermeable enough to hold intact the immensities of my perception.

* * *

1 July, 1946